THE GIFT OF A VIRGIN

Lina M. Fruzzetti

•

RUTGERS UNIVERSITY PRESS

New Brunswick, New Jersey

THE GIFT OF A VIRGIN

Women, Marriage, and Ritual in a Bengali Society

Library of Congress Cataloging in Publication Data

Fruzzetti, Lina.
The gift of a virgin.

Bibliography: p.
Includes index.
1. Women, Bengali—India—West Bengal. 2. Marriage customs and rites, Hindu—India—West Bengal. 3. Women, Hindu—India—West Bengal. 4. West Bengal (India)—Social life and customs. I. Title.
DS432.B4F78 305.4'8 81-15337
ISBN 0-8135-0939-4 AACR2

To Kebedesh Tezba, my mother

CONTENTS

Appendix B
The Order of Strī Ācārs

Appendix C
Sociological Studies of Indian Women

PREFACE

This book is the result of four years of field research carried out in the subdivisional town of Vishnupur, District of Bankura, West Bengal. Research was made possible by grants from the Foreign Area Fellowship Program (SSRC, New York) and from the American Institute of Indian Studies. I would like to thank these two institutions for their generous support.

To the people of Vishnupur and especially to the women of the town, I owe a special gratitude: their hospitality, patience, and constant attention facilitated my research project. I cannot mention all the people who helped me, but the numerous marriages and birth and death rituals I have attended indicate the extent to which the people of Vishnupur shared their lives with me. I will single out Srimati Minu Bhattacharya and the Mohila Samity, Sri Maniklal Sinha and his household, and Sri Rabindranath Ghosh and his *jñati,* to whom I owe a special debt. Dr. Ashutosh Bhattacharya kindly sponsored my research project and I extend my thanks to him. To my many, many *māsīmā*s (MZ), *pisīmā*s (FZ), *didimā*s (FM), and *boudi*s (eBW), I owe much gratitude for the hours they spent teaching me about Bengali life and the value of women in society and for making fieldwork a very enjoyable experience. I would also like to thank the government officials in the District of Bankura, who were very cordial, encouraging, and helpful at all times.

William Rowe and Steve Gudeman read earlier drafts of this manuscript and made some excellent suggestions. I am greatly indebted to my advisor and friend William Rowe, who guided my field inquiry and extended his assistance and friendship during the period of writing this book. Bill Rowe was also very supportive during the writing of my thesis and removed daily obstacles as much as possible to allow me to write. He deserves a very special thanks. Marilyn H. Fetterman and Ákos Östör helped me edit the manuscript and suggested stylistic changes.

I owe a special place in this preface to my husband, Ákos Östör, and to my two little daughters. My study of ritual activities of Hindu and Muslim women complemented his work on a similar subject from a male perspective. The complementary nature of the research has already triggered several publications by the two of us. Ákos encouraged me to continue with the research on women at a time when the subject was not fashionable. He helped me in the field and throughout the arduous time of writing. Leila (then Koko) was born at the right time for me to be accepted as a full woman by Bengalis and to be included in their midst during specific rituals. I thank her for the assistance that she offered in her capacity as a child. Katyayini was my inspiration for actually writing the book, and her birth was equally auspicious. The two girls and their father made it happen.

My mother is the last mentioned, and to her the book is dedicated. She has been a continuing inspiration to me. Although she and the women in her family were not formally educated, she has given me—as a woman—unconditional encouragement to pursue long, expensive professional training. I hope that she will find it worthwhile and find reason to look into the future. I dedicate the results of my work to her.

Sand paintings used ornamentally on the title page and chapter openings are *alpanā* designs, which form a part of ritual narratives (*brata rathā*), prevalent in rural Bengal. *Alpanās* are an important feature of women's rituals (the *strī ācārs*). They are reproduced here by courtesy of the Santiniretan School, Chitrangsu Institute of Art and Handicraft, Santiniketan, India.

Symbols Used

B	brother	S	son
D	daughter	W	wife
F	father	Z	sister
H	husband	e	elder
M	mother	y	younger

THE GIFT OF A VIRGIN

The bride and groom after completion of the first day's marriage ritual.

INTRODUCTION

This study is concerned with marriage in Bengali society, particularly the actions and meanings of marriage as they relate to women. I analyze Bengali society through the perspective of the indigenous domain of women's activities—the relationships, in local terms, among women as a separable whole, their household and kinship groups, life cycle rituals and beliefs, and especially the symbols of marriage. Of crucial importance in constructing women's roles and statuses in the context of their own world is the problem of deciphering the meanings underlying the exchanges and rituals surrounding marriage, of finding meaning within the relation between social action and cultural symbolism.

Recent anthropological studies emphasizing the problems of meaning in social relations range widely in perspective: among others, there are the formal logic of Lévi-Strauss (1966), the creation of meaning in event and process in Geertz (1973), the study of dramatic expression in ritual as a resolution of fundamental social tensions in Turner (1967), the account of an indigenous system of symbols and domains in Schneider (1968, 1972, 1976), and the combination of indigenous ideology with morphology in the structural and historical studies of Dumont (1970a, 1970b). It is within this broad concern for the meaning of social actions that this study is situated.

My purpose is to examine the meanings of social actions by emphasizing the cultural and symbolic dimension of society and by analyzing local Bengali social relations in terms of particular concepts, categories, and symbols. Given this intent, my analysis deals with a series of questions largely ignored in anthropological studies of India: if the domain of women's activities is a separate one, how is it structured, understood, and expressed in the context of the wider society; is there articulation between these levels of Bengali society; is the women's world in opposition, contradiction, or complementarity to society as a whole;[1] what are the principles that organize and interpret the domain of women's social relations; do these contribute to our understanding of Bengali society in ways neglected by previous caste, kinship, and religious studies?

With the exception of work by Gupta (1974) and Yalman (1962,

1963, 1967), studies of kinship and marriage in India have treated women as a mere appendage to research.[2] Most studies of household, caste, kinship, marriage, and religion in India have researched a segmentary society as if it were a whole and have assumed that the study of women's domain is not separable and therefore would contribute nothing to the understanding of the larger society. These studies make *a priori* assumptions about the women's world and decide in terms of Western perceptions what the roles of women are in terms of the household, the private domain, and the kitchen versus the public domain, men, politics, and caste. Yet in India the relation between male and female may not be contrary, contradictory, or oppositional: it may be a complementary relationship extending from a separate woman's domain to the other levels of society as well.

In the West, the position of Asian women is generally assumed to be one of subjection and domination by men. This suppression is said to be maintained and justified by religion. Yet the complementarity of the male and female principles is one of the basic tenets of Hindu philosophy and Hindu perception of the world (Fruzzetti, 1971: 6–7). The position of Indian women today is assumed to be parallel to that of women in nineteenth-century Western societies. My own point of view is based on the subjective orientation of the actor in society; hence, to me such seemingly objective comparisons err by overlooking the cultural understanding of women.

This study is the result of my fieldwork in rural West Bengal. The first time I did fieldwork there in the subdivisional town of Vishnupur was from 1967 to 1969. That initial research concerned the Muslims of the town, their social organization, marriage, kinship, and the role of Islam in their lives. The work centered on Muslim women and public festivals within the Muslim community. Since I was particularly interested in the role of Islam and the position of minorities in a secular state, Vishnupur was an ideal place for the research. My fieldwork on a second stay there, from 1971 to 1973, was devoted to the ritual activities of caste Hindu and Muslim Bengali women.[3] This study is the result of a small part of the research material. For lack of space and time, I have chosen to write about Hindú marriage ritual here and to save other related material on Muslim Bengali rituals for future publications. (Bengali Hindu and Muslim women share similarities in parts of their ritual domain, the similarities to be understood in terms of "Bengali culture"; but at the same time, significant differences are also present.)

My research was divided into two parts. The first stage of fieldwork was a study of women's culture and models for action (the indigenous view of women's role) in general terms throughout the town. The second stage concentrated on household roles of women, the domain of women's rituals, the role of women in life cycle rites (*bratas*), the economy, and politics. The network of neighborhood relationships among women of different households was also researched in an endeavor to isolate variables according to caste and class. The last phase of the study, which overlapped the second somewhat, included the public roles of women: their participation in major rituals organized and celebrated by men as well as the role of their associations in the town, including various religious sects, their involvement in politics, production, and cooperatives. I also examined attempts to advance the position of women in the society and culture of the town; education; health schemes; and the attitudes of educated women to traditional views of women and to the maintenance of tradition itself.

It is, as would seem obvious, easier for a woman anthropologist to gain access to information and data about women than for a man. Yet, any outsider to rural Indian society is an intruder into a world of rituals, beliefs, household economy, and kinship and marriage ties and might be expected to be treated as such. Entry here differs drastically from entry into urban Indian society. I had no problem, however, in doing research with Bengali women; there was no hostility, and often embarrassingly immense hospitality. This was, in part, due to my previous two years of fieldwork, during which rapport was established that led to this later continuance of old relationships.

The main problem in working with women in rural areas was that interviewing could only be carried out during the hottest time of day, noon to about 3 P.M. (when women were not busy preparing food or doing other household chores). However, on special occasions, the celebrations of life cycle rites, women did not follow the daily household routine. At these times women were busy preparing the relevant rituals of the *saṃskāras*. I observed and discussed these preparations and performances and participated when I was asked to. Being a married woman with a small child, I was auspicious in the eyes of the women and many times was asked to make up the number of women needed to perform the rituals, especially at marriage.

The first step was the observation of household rituals (*pūjās*), the washing of the line's (*baṇgśas*) deities (*kuladebatās*). This included the observation of rituals in various social divisions, subcastes, and households. It also included the rites pertaining to different statuses of women: virgin, widow, married woman. Here I noted the roles of women in the *pūjā*s of the 'line' and in the major public rituals and festivals. I took slides and photographs of all these rituals and recorded the narrative, the manner of the performance, who participates, how and when, who is absent and why and when, the objects used for performances, and what was being done and recited. I kept track of whether the action was a part of a larger ritual and who the deities were that were being worshipped. In short, I tried to find as many variations in as many contexts as possible so as to avoid simplifying the cultural system through inadequate coverage of events.

Much of what seemed meaningless became clear in the second phase of my research—through discussions with participants singly and in groups. These were open-ended conversations as well as structured interviews, involving at times two groups of women, from middle or high and low castes. Long interviews and discussions with the ritual participants led to answers and further queries which were discussed yet again. New problems emerged as old ones were cleared up. Sometimes problems encountered in one household were resolved by another.

In this way, I pieced together missing elements in the explanations of rituals, translated actions into appropriate meanings, formulated questions which were not idiosyncratic to particular persons, and deduced answers which were agreed to by most in a particular role, function, or group. The household was the initial unit of investigation. Then the household was taken together with its extended members, those living in a different house, those related in terms of other groupings (blood or marriage, subcaste, locality, and so forth). The next and more difficult part concerned the cross-cutting and overlapping relations among different groups and the categorization of the rituals of these groups, beginning with the household and extending beyond that unit to the community of the whole town. Research of this sort proved to be long and arduous. Yet it was very useful for establishing a woman's domain of action in relation to other social domains and other group divisions. When questions of hierarchy were involved, it was also necessary to gain permission for entry from each group. In this way, I could tell caste variations from household differences and could see similarities in the actions of women that cut across all other divisions and groupings.

The third phase (which may have been a unique field method at the time) was the use of slide shows, during which I taped questions and commentaries by women on a running but unobserved tape recorder. Seeing themselves enact rituals on slides and Super-8 movies was a new and exciting phenomenon for many women. While showing sequential slides, I asked questions about the rituals: what was being done, what was being used, what was being recited and why, and so forth. All through the interview, the recorder captured the running commentaries, exegeses, and explanations. The reason for keeping the recorder out of sight was that some women found it difficult (out of shyness and a fear of the machine) to speak into the microphone. With the machine out of sight, but with the knowledge that it was there, a wealth of information was made accessible, including arguments among women on certain topics, answers and questions about the differences between the same rituals in various households and caste groups. Complete exegeses of ritual objects and actions were taped. Indigenous categories and concepts thus elicited became useful in attempting a cultural analysis of the rituals.

Fieldwork was not entirely spent in observation, collection of data, participation in ritual action, and elicitation of explanations. I also spent time in the day-to-day activities of households, being with women dressing, washing, and feeding the very young and the elderly, cleaning and cooking, performing the daily household worship. Many hours were spent each day watching and learning women's activities and lore: what is cooked in what season, month, day, or time of day; what food items are used for what ritual; what is used to cure illness and how. All of these lessons were related to systems of belief and action as women saw and understood them. These were very enjoyable times—gossiping with women in the cookhouses; learning about their ancestors, father's house, in-laws' house; finding out who was getting married, giving birth, and so forth. These were also times for exchanging ideas, for comparing different cultural systems of beliefs and meanings. The style and quality of life is not only to be learned but to be experienced. Only in this way can an anthropologist act as an outsider (researcher, investigator) and, equally important, as an insider, a member part of the society in question inasmuch as the local system and one's personality allow this.

My attempt to analyze Bengali society as a whole is in the French sociological tradition and follows the dictates of a sociological apperception of man in society: individuals are recognized as empirical beings and members of groups. I view these ties as being culturally formed and understood, suspending persons and groups in relation to each other in a web of meaning (Dumont, 1970a: 21–63; Geertz, 1973; Östör, Fruzzetti, and Barnett, 1980: chap. 3). These webs of meanings are accessible to analysis and interpretation since they are expressed and understood through symbols and cultural categories of belief and ritual, power and status, economy and politics, kinship and marriage as these are culturally constructed in particular given societies.

Bengali women constitute a world with its own separate rules as well as its relation to the wider society. This domain is expressed most clearly in women's rituals, *meyeder ācār*s (customs, habits, and actions of women), which are restricted to and conducted by women—as opposed to the rituals of the wider society (the *pūjā*s, or festivals) where Brāhmaṇ priests officiate. What these rituals express constitutes a subculture in Bengal, giving meaning to the separate activities and lives of women in relation to Bengali culture as a whole. This domain of social actions and symbolic expressions has its relation to other locally defined domains: kinship, marriage, politics, ritual, and bazaar economy. In effect, Bengal society as a whole cannot be understood without exploring the relations between these domains and the world of women.

Although this study is not specifically about caste or kinship, it does relate to these general problems of Indian sociology. Kinship, marriage, and caste relations are complementary to the indigenous meanings of femaleness and womanhood. The principles of hierarchy, purity and impurity, maleness and femaleness are fundamental to the understanding of Indian society, and it is through an analysis of women's ritual activities—specifically marriage rituals (*strī ācār*s)—that these principles become fully accessible and meaningful.

Some may find it unorthodox to shift, seemingly arbitrarily, from women, marriage, rituals, and the sacred to 'line,' *jāti* (caste), and marriage exchanges (the sacred gift of the virgin and gifts of goods), and only then to *strī ācār*s. But there is logic to my presentation: I am primarily concerned with women in marriage and other rituals, but I intentionally reverse the traditional social-structural approach to Indian societies. My aim is not to separate gift exchanges in marriages (as economic), caste and kinship relations (as social structure), rituals and beliefs (as Hindu religion) but to consider aspects of these relationships as constituted, unified, in a cultural domain, and thus to seek the meaning of actions and symbols. This is the reason for the way my argument unfolds. In order to situate the discussion of marriage rituals, and so to gain understanding of women's domain, I first place marriage and the status of women within locally conceived and given contexts. It is at this point that it becomes possible to analyze the indigenous terms of sacredness (as a Bengali concept, not opposed to the "profane" in the Durkheimian sense). Next I link the separation of categories in marriage to relationships in general (kinship, blood, line, caste), since marriage (and its rites) cannot be treated as an isolated entity but only as part of other domains. Thus, in discussing dowry and other gifts, I also clarify the notions and actions of relatives. Similarly, in dealing with marriage rituals, the importance of caste, hierarchy, and exchange emerge, thus highlighting the nature of Hindu society. In the course of these discussions I present the women's domain in relation to the two kinds of gifts—bride and dowry—and only then is the reader ready to approach the *strī ācār*s in detail. In the text, I have grouped the marriage rituals (*strī ācār*s) according to broad categories contextually situated rather than diachronically performed. Common themes run through the *ācār*s, but these commonalities can only be appreciated if the meanings themselves are grouped. *Ācār*s as used, practiced, and understood by women are a fundamental interpretation of the symbolism of marriage and the ambiguous in-between roles of women as wives and daughters. (See Appendix B for a diachronic description of *strī ācār*s as performed.)

Chapter 1 presents both an ethnographic and an analytical case for separating the gift of the virgin from the marriage dowry. This approach highlights the link between prestations, relatives by blood (*bhāiyat* and *baṇgśa*) and relatives by marriage (*kuṭum*), caste (*jāti*) system, the intricacies of an indigenous alliance system, and the meaning of femaleness in Bengali society. Chapter 2 describes how the five *mugla*s, the *kanyā kañjali* rituals, and the different gift exchanges in marriage all structure and articulate caste and kinship principles. Here I examine the cultural meanings of gifts. The same chapter considers the *ācār*s dealing directly with gifts and prestations. Chapter 3 narrates married women's rituals, *strī ācār*s themselves, and demonstrates the meaning and significance of these rituals for all Bengali women. I also examine women's roles as wives and daughters of lines, as evident in the symbolism of the rituals. The rituals are grouped into those offered to deities; those performed for the blessings of the couple; and the *ācār*s performed by the bride and groom themselves. All three sets of *strī ācār*s specifically enact and reaffirm women's roles and statuses in society. In chapter 4 I discuss the changes in the status of women through marriage and delineate the principles and the structuring of caste and kinship groups. The volume ends with the conclusions drawn from the study.

CHAPTER 1

Sampradān: *The Gift of Women and the Status of Men*

Hindu marriage is a sacred (*pabittra*) rite linking persons to groups in terms of indigenous principles of and for action (where marriage, sacred ritual, person, and group are culturally constructed). Marriage also affects the meaning of the relationships among and between persons and groups, and the meanings of the categories to which these relationships refer (or, conversely, the locally understood relationships expressed by terms, symbols, and categories). More generally, marriage is one aspect of Bengali notions and practices built around birth and descent. Marriage is entered into and performed to ensure the immortality, continuity, and purity of the male descent line and of the social group for which the line is the organizing principle. Marriage is vital to the maintenance of one's caste status, defined as one's standing among the smaller segmentary subdivisions within the caste. The principles of marriage practice are therefore inseparable from the principles of hierarchy at the very core of Indian society. Marriage relationships as the creation and maintenance of male lines, defined in terms of Bengali concepts, ideas, and categories, are a separable domain of action. At the same time, marriage is linked to other domains, such as economic exchange and politicoeconomic power. Marriage is also linked to process and hierarchy, to belief and ritual; it is marriage as the link between the sacred and purity that yields hierarchy. In the following sections I explore some of these relationships through the construction of Bengali meanings and practices in marriage.

Marriage is one of the major life cycle rituals and is related to other rites in the cycle of a person's life. There are parallels between birth and marriage in the form of the ritual action, the deities involved, the number of items used, and the participating ritualists and kin groups of bloodline and prior marriages. But unlike birth (and death), the beliefs and rituals surrounding marriage are linked to all Bengali myths and rites, whether or not these have to do with the life cycle. Marriage alters not only a woman's status and group affiliation but also all her future actions. The rituals not only express these realities but define, construct, and interpret them for the actors themselves. A newly married woman begins a new style of life, observing her in-laws' customs and norms of action. Most important, she adopts her *śvaśur ghar*'s (in-laws' house's) observance of purity and pollution in regard to the major life cycle and other sacred rituals (*saṃskāra*s and *pūjā*s).

Marriage is also the key for distinguishing *kuṭum* from *jñati* classes of relatives: *kuṭum* are relatives by marriage; *jñati* are relatives in the male line. The gathering of relatives at marriages serves to reinforce existing kinship ties and to welcome a whole new set of lines to an ongoing alliance system composed of a number of marriage cycles eventually affecting the caste group as a whole. The elaborate rituals not only order, separate, and unite different groups of relatives but initiate, create, and integrate an entirely new line—that of groom and bride—into a complex system of alliances, bringing the lines of the in-laws into a wider social system.

Bengali marriage (*biye*) consists of two major elements: the gift of a virgin (*sampradān*) and the payment of a dowry (*pon*). The gift of a virgin is a ritual of purely sacred connotation. Dowry preceeds the marriage ritual itself and is an activity which can be understood in economic terms alone. In this study I am concerned with this dual mode of exchange in the marriage system, particularly the ways it brings together the sacred and the nonsacred in the hierarchical system of a caste society. As my discussion of the Bengali concepts expressed in marriage rituals continues, it will become evident that I am analyzing two different modes of exchange, the giving and the taking of gifts, both of which take place at the same time in the marriage ceremonies. I hope also to clarify how concepts such as *pon* (dowry), *dābi* (a rightful, obligatory gift), *dān* (a bestowal, a "perfect" gift), and *paona* (a gift given for services, one which ought to be paid to the givers of services) involve a number of kin (in bloodline and in marriage), caste brothers, and others. Furthermore, I explain how these exchanges and rituals structure the society in terms of indigenous principles such as purity and hierarchy and how they integrate the domains of kinship and of economic and political relations with the beliefs and rites surrounding marriage.

To understand the full difference between traditional Hindu marriage and marriage in other societies, including our own, I begin by discussing the two opposing forms of marriage in Bengali society—sacred, Hindu marriage and nonsacred, controversial, "love-marriage," or court-registered marriage.[1] This contrast becomes all the more instructive since it involves different aspects of categories such as love, marriage, and devotion. After comparing the two types of marriage, my discussion clarifies the importance of *strī ācār*s and also the role of marriage institutions in creating new relations and reaffirming alliances.

Controversial Marriages: Sacred and Nonsacred Love

Marriages not performed in the Hindu ritual manner are often referred to as "love-marriage" or "love *biye*." The use of the English term indicates the lack of an appropriate Bengali term. There is an indigenous term for 'love,' *prem,* meaning the conjugal love of husband and wife, but when it is used outside the sacred context it refers to adultery; carnality; nonsacred, physical, antisocial love. Marriages involving brides and grooms of different castes, within forbidden degrees of kinship relationship, and of different communities (such as Hindu, Muslim, or Christian) are also referred to as love-marriages, as are marriages undertaken either in defiance of parents and caste brothers or as political gestures against Brahmanic "superstition."

Love-marriages are considered immoral (*khārāp,* "bad"), and according to consensus the Bengali *samāj* (society) of a town would not consent to such marriages.[2] Traditional marriages in India are always arranged marriages performed by priests (Brāhmaṇ ritualists), while love marriages tend to be intercaste marriages performed in a court by a civil judge. Love-marriages generally create turmoil at all points of the hierarchical, segmentary caste society; but they particularly affect members of the couple's households and kin groups, since love-marriages breach caste and kinship principles. Old men and women of the town blame the current politicoeconomic situation, the modern world, college education, and Hindi cinema for the occasionally "outrageous" behavior of young people. In cases of love-marriages, the parents of the couple and the immediate male-line members of the household are pressured by people of the neighborhood (*pāṛā*) and members of the same caste living in the town to take a stand against the marriage by cutting off all relations with the offending couple. Even though the couple's parents are prepared to forgive their children for committing an act which is in direct contradiction to the ideals of *samāj*, pressures force them to bar the offending couple from their house (though a brother may try to visit his sister privately). The household members have to live in the local Hindu or Bengali *samāj* and to continue to interact with other members of their caste group. The offending couple's presence in the town is a constant reminder to the townsmen of the breach in caste principles, and the tension between the offender and the rest of the *samāj* is always felt. Brothers and sisters of the couple may be affected by such a marriage, becoming ineligible for marriage with "good houses."

In one case of love-marriage in Vishnupur, a Śaṅkari (conch-shell-maker—an artisan caste) girl married a Kāyastha (scribe—a caste of writers and clerks) boy, both of whom were in government employment. Though the Śaṅkaris are a much lower caste group in the caste hierarchy than the Kāyastha, the marriage outraged the girl's caste members more than those of the boy. The marriage was cause enough for the local Śaṅkaris to cast out and cut off all possible relationships with the girl. Her own brother and father's brother initiated the breaking of relations with her, and the move encouraged the rest of the Śaṅkaris to do the same.

This case of the Śaṅkari-Kāyastha love-marriage had some complicating circumstances which reveal contrasts as well as accommodations to traditional and love-marriages today. Both the bride and groom had been adopted while children by a Brāhmaṇ woman.[3] The girl was already in her mid-thirties, past the accepted marriage age, and she had neither wealth nor property of her own. The marriage was arranged by their adopted Brāhmaṇ mother. After the marriage the Śaṅkaris would not acknowledge the girl's marriage to a higher caste than their own. But the main reason the girl became an outcaste from the Śaṅkari caste was that she had scorned caste principles. At the birth of her daughter a year later, no one would perform the rituals of the mother's brother. In the future the little girl's caste affiliation and status will be open to doubt; she will not be accepted by a Śaṅkari man as a wife, and it was generally suspected that a Kāyastha boy would not want to marry her either.

Unmarried girls normally agree with the choice of a groom made by the male members of their household. Very few girls would present an argument in defense of love-marriage, even though such marriages are their family's only recourse if they wish to avoid paying the large dowries demanded by eligible men who are well placed in marriage circles within the caste. This economizing argument is used to justify love-marriages after the fact, especially when the couple are both of the same caste but of markedly different status. Yet, even in these cases, love-marriages risk one's kin and caste ties and, perhaps more significantly, challenge the male line, the members of the line, the household, and one's relatives in the building of further relationships through subsequent marriages. Marriages initiated and completed by unmarried girls without the consent of the men and the women of their household are not the type of union Bengali caste-society takes as its ideal.

The important term in love-marriage is love, or *prem*. The construct emphasizes a certain aspect of *prem* as the sole basis for marriage. Though *prem* is an aspect of traditional Hindu marriages, the notion of love does not initiate or act as the mainspring of the traditional marriage relation, and it does not play any role in the marriage negotiations. Hindu marriage unites the son and daughter of two separate houses and lines where the protagonists are often unknown to each other. *Prem* is, on the other hand, the exclusive basis of love-marriage; and townspeople regard such a union as cheap and immoral, destined to fail because of its very foundation: the illusory and impermanent nature of *prem*. Hindu marriages take place regardless of the couple expressing like or dislike, love or hatred, of each other. Often the bride and groom do not see each other before the marriage. Bengalis stress that *prem* is a part of the husband–wife tie, but that love has to develop through time, growing in and through the *swāmī strī* (husband–wife) relationship. Bengali marriages are not devoid of love, but *prem* is not the main reason for the union.

Prem and *Bhakti*

Prem is love, but it carries different meanings in different social contexts. When Bengalis say that love-marriages are motivated by *prem*, the term denotes more than a romantic relationship. Here the emphasis is on "*prem* as sex alone," as if the couple's only aim is to enjoy sexual relations without *biye*. The two kinds of marriage differ on this point. Marriages negotiated by the parents and performed by the priests (Brāhmaṇ Pūjāri) are not for the fulfillment of one's sexual expectations. Sex is part of Hindu marriage, but it is neither the immediate nor ultimate aim. *Prem* in *biye* is sacred conjugal love, but in and by itself, *prem karā* (making love) is antisocial and dangerous in the way it challenges the caste and kinship principles in a hierarchical society. *Prem* in this sense is contrary to the principles of purity and lineality.

Prem is an integral Hindu notion. *Prem bhakti* (love and devotion)—a combination of worship and love as in the relation between gods and persons—characterizes the devotional cults of the Vaiṣṇava sects. Kṛṣṇa's *prem bhakti,* the relation between the devotee and a personal god, is the model for the relationship between husband (*swāmī,* lord), and wife (*strī*) in marriage. Marriage is a relationship of *prem* and *bhog* (acceptance, referring to both suffering and enjoyment); it is hierarchical and reciprocal at the same time. The husband should love and respect (*prem bhog* and *sammān*) his wife, for he is lord; and the wife should be devoted (*bhakti*) to her godlike husband. *Prem* is used for both types of marriage, sacred and nonsacred, but with a difference in emphasis. *Prem* in the traditional sense is linked to respect (*sammān*) and, on another level, to the notion of *bhakti* or devotional love. Though a newly married couple's marriage is arranged and negotiated, they are expected to show each other all the signs of *sammān.* The husband should care for and protect his wife, while the wife should look to her *swāmī* as her personal deity, to whom she offers and shares her *prem* on two levels, devotional and conjugal.

Lest it be thought strange that conjugal love should also be regarded as divine love, it should be noted that there is no clearcut division between men and the gods in Hindu ideologies. Deities, incarnate gods, god-kings, and ancestors are all sacred, divine beings, related respectively to different levels of action in society. They are all worthy of worship. This is also true of Brāhmaṇs, *gurus*, family priests, and fathers, who are on the continuum between gods and mere persons. Similarly, the husband should be addressed with devotion by his wife. The groom is regarded and treated as a deity at a particular stage of the marriage ritual. The bride herself becomes a goddess at another juncture, bride and groom representing the Lord Rāmā and his faithful wife, Sitā. All these relationships are aspects of the complex *prem bhakti* tie—the hierarchy of the constituting units changing from one case to the other and from level to level. To say that a wife will treat her husband as a deity only means that she can begin his worship instead of taking up worship of other deities. A woman's husband is her first god. A married woman begins her day by touching her husband's feet (*praṇām karā*—a sign of respect) before she even steps down from her bed.

In the same way that a woman's husband is her *guru,* the husband's mother and father and all elder members of the household are *gurujan* to a young bride. The relation of a young wife (*boumā*) to elders in her in-laws' house is one of *lajjā* (avoidance, meaning shyness or shame). In front of her *śvaśur śāsuṛī* (father-in-law and mother-in-law) the incoming woman must cover her head with the end part of her *sāri* as part of the avoidance relationship. Women are shy and embarrassed about being married, since being married means a woman has sexual relations with her husband. It is sex, an act performed not for desire and enjoyment, but mainly for the creation of children and the continuation of the *baṇgśa* (male line), that makes women ashamed.

Sex is not discussed in the household, especially not in the company of one's elders. During the first day of the marriage (the day when the couple stays up all night) the younger members of the house gather in the *bāsar ghar,* the room where the bride and groom stay, and tell lewd jokes and tease the newly married couple in sexual terms. Women who stand in a "mother's relation" to the girls in the house—with the exception of the grandmother—cannot stay and listen to these jokes, since elders must receive respect from the younger members of the house, not only in being served and attended to but by not being submitted to foul language. A young bride will always be shy and express the *lajjā* in front of her in-laws during the first years of marriage. There are still some houses where the woman will talk to her husband only when they are alone, which in most cases is just at night.

In sum, Bengali Hindu marriage expresses devotional and physical love; the husband is both a deity and a male companion from whom one conceives children to continue the *baṇgśa.* Continuation of the husband's *baṇgśa* is the aim of marriage, the reason for bringing about the alliance of the two lines and households which contract the marriage. Love-marriage, however, expresses the other aspect of traditional marriage, the sexual relationship of the couple, making the carnal experience itself the end and basis of marriage. Because of the difference between the two marriages, one accepted and the other rejected by the *samāj,* guardians of unmarried girls go so far as to sell their paddy fields, use up their savings, and sell their wives' jewelry to procure a good groom for their daughters.

Marriage Rites and Beliefs

There is more to the institution of marriage than mere change of status; otherwise love-marriage could be accommodated more easily. Married love, however, is not secular and develops along the lines of a devotional, respectful, and conjugal relationship between husband and wife. In the traditional marriage ritual the priest follows the sacred texts (Śāstras). The rite is witnessed by men and women as well as by the gods above and around, including the ancestors of the *ghar* (house). Lord Nārāyan (Viṣṇu) is called upon to be the major witness of the marriage at *āgni sakkhī* (fire witness) when the couple, hands clasped together, pour *khoi* (a kind of fried pulse) into the *homa* (sacrificial fire). All relatives of both bride and groom are invited to the marriage rituals: the *bār jātri* ('groom's journey') are those who accompany the groom to the bride's house, where the marriage is performed, and the *jātri pakkha* (the 'bride's side') are the bride's father's *jñati* and *kuṭum.*

Hindu marriage is also more than just the rituals performed by the priest. In addition, a number of equally important rites not recorded in the sacred texts are performed and are relevant for understanding the role of married women in the household. The purpose of these *strī ācār*s is to exemplify to the bride and the groom the meaning and importance of *saṇgsār,* the activities of daily life.

*Strī ācār*s provide reflections of the world of women through their own point of view, a world which can be understood only in its own terms. The *ācār*s ask *maṅgal kāmonā* (blessings) for the newly married couple, blessings from *ghar* members, other relatives, and neighborhood people. The *strī ācār*s encompass one's own relations, *pāṛā* (neighborhood) people, one's own caste, and other caste women—all these ties understood through a woman's notion of alliance. *Strī ācār*s, then, reenact and symbolize the *saṇgsār* to the bride and groom and at the same time reinforce the couple's ties with neighbors, relatives, and caste brothers.

The marriage rite brings together different categories and groups of people. This is the occasion to assemble all the closely related male lines and all the relatives by marriage of the male lines. Friends, neighbors, and the local caste groups are also invited. All kinds of bonds are reaffirmed. Marriage circles are rendered visible and future alliances discussed.

Once the date of marriage is settled, invitations are sent to *jñati* (male-line relatives) and *kuṭum* (marriage relatives), including one's married daughters' and sons' *śvaśur bāṛi* (in-laws' house) people and relatives by marriage of both bride and groom on the father's and the mother's side. Not all of one's *baṇgśa* (relatives of the male line of a house, people with whom one shares both blood and *gotra*—the maximal descent identification label from an ancestor in the male line—or *gotra* alone) live in the same place so they must be sent invitations. (Only one's immediate blood relatives, grandparents from the father's side, father's brothers, and their wives and children usually reside together.) Special arrangements and welcome are extended to one's *kuṭum*. This is the time to show them respect and honor by feeding and treating them well, since they are the group to whom one gives daughters and to whom one is therefore indebted, the indebtedness being made very clear on these occasions. Gifts and prestations are made to the people of one's married daughter's house; the father-in-law pays special respect to the *jāmāi* (son-in-law) of that house, and only then can he attend to his own future son-in-law.

Marriage, then, is a time to continue the pattern of giving and receiving gifts. Ceremonies also serve to bring *beyān* and *beyāy* (the parents of a previously married bride and groom) together. This further strengthens the existing marriage networks and may bring about future alliances. Since all closely related male lines and *kuṭum* are assembled, marriages serve as an occasion to inquire among one's relatives about the availability of a good *patra* (groom) or *kanyā* (bride) for one's unmarried children.

The marriage rites also strengthen the *jajmani* (system of service), a scheme for the division of labor, economic reciprocity, and redistribution of goods and services in caste society. A household receives services throughout the year from representatives of various castes: barber (Nāpit), washerman (Dhobā), midwife (Dāimā), priest (Brāhmaṇ Pūjāri), musician (Dom). Barber and priest have important duties in the marriage ritual. But all service-caste persons associated with the *jajmān* household are invited and given gifts and food.

As one comes to understand the meaning of marriage in Bengal, the resentment of love-marriage also becomes comprehensible. Love creates and destroys at the same time. Love-marriage is a meaningless type of union in the local scheme since it does not accomplish what a traditional marriage is meant to accomplish. Love-marriage is a one-sided affair; it unites two people but separates them from their caste brothers and close relatives. The activities surrounding traditional marriage ties create new alliances and lines, strengthen past ties with *kuṭum*, link the provider of sacred ritual services to the recipient household, and fulfill obligations to deities and ancestors (*pitṛ puruṣ*). One's ancestors (*pitṛ* and *mātṛ*, father's and mother's side) are offered water oblations (*jal deoyā*) on this day. The ancestors are asked to attend the marriage, and their *maṅgal kāmonā* (blessings) are sought for the young couple. For people of the town, marriage in the traditional sense reaffirms previous relationships and establishes new ones.

The Gift of the Virgin in Relation to Caste and Kinship Principles

Sampradān is a father's gift of his daughter to a groom in the context of marriage (*biye*) rituals, the offering being mediated by the Brāhmaṇ priest. This makes the groom into a son-in-law (*jāmāi*) of the bride's house and the bride into a "wife-mother" (*boumā*) and daughter-in-law of the groom's house. The gift is made through a series of rites and incantations. Here, I discuss the symbolism of the ritual in terms of indigenous culture and in relation to the actions of persons and groups participating in the ceremonies and with particular attention to the categories and relationships of women as the rituals develop and move to a resolution. The question of participants raises the problem of defining the "who" in the sociological task of finding out what is being done and who does it. Marriage rules reflect the Bengali construction and meaning of the person, the way persons are created, and the matter of who can marry whom. Discussing marriage rules is in fact discussing an indigenous domain of kinship.

A father cannot give his daughter to certain categories of relatives. Close relatives—especially blood relatives—are ineligible for marriage. Thus, the first Bengali marriage rule: there cannot be a marriage alliance between two *ghar*s whose members share blood. Blood relatives are persons in the male lines of one's father and mother with the blood tie counted back to the seventh generation on the father's side and to the third generation on the mother's side. Outside these seventh-degree and third-degree relationships, one is free to marry "relatives" provided they do not have the same *gotra*. Accordingly, those with whom one shares blood include one's FB-FZ and their children, MB-MZ and their children, making BS, FBS, MBS ineligible as marriage partners for one's daughter. On the other hand, a daughter's daughter's daughter may marry into the original line since she has a different *gotra* and is coming in from an entirely different male line; she is not a *jñati* (which is a group of male-linked relatives not marriageable under any circumstances).

The greatest gift a man can bestow, the one from which he acquires the most merit (*punya*), is the gift of his daughter in marriage. Hence there is an insistence on the proper observance of the ways in which the gift ought to be made. Complementing the exclusion of blood relatives is the rule that marriage must be within one's own *jāti* (caste) group. Further considerations lead to the rules of avoidance of the MZ's line and to concepts such as *bhāiyat, sapiṇḍa, sāt-*

puruṣ, and *śuddhatā* (purity). Not only are the person and the idea of the person born through marriage, but the social order itself rests on the principles symbolized and expressed in the rituals surrounding marriage and in the actions leading up to the *sampradān*. Both hierarchical relations of caste and the immortality of the line and the ancestors rest on marriage practices. Caste being a segmentary hierarchical system, some of its constituent units are necessarily of equal status; and so they are opposed, in a structure, to other units of inferior or superior status. Marriages constitute lines and ensure immortality. Thus caste and kinship are inseparable; marriages mediate between lines, maintaining equivalence within the larger system of caste hierarchy.

Bhāiyat, Sātpuruṣ, Sapiṇḍa, and Pollution

Bhāiyat are close, living male relatives, members of the segmentary collection of *baṇgśa*s (lines) going back from ego to the seventh generation (*sātpuruṣ*). Both terms refer to males, *bhāiyat* (literally, 'group of brothers') being related to brother (*bhāi*), and *puruṣ* meaning "male ancestor," though both terms also encompass the incoming wives of the line. All these persons are affected by birth and death pollution occurring anywhere in the line. Pollution (*aśauc*) has to be removed according to certain practices common to the *bhāiyat* as a whole. Just as purity is shared throughout the *bhāiyat*, so too is impurity, though the severity of pollution decreases with increasing distance of relationship from those among whom a birth or death has occurred. The *bhāiyat* share blood or *gotra* or both. The inmarrying women share *gotra* only. Thus blood is not the exclusive basis for defining *bhāiyat* and *baṇgśa*s.

Married women follow the purity and pollution rules of their husband's *bhāiyat* rather than those of their father's. Incoming women and one's own daughters are equally affected by pollution. Death is more polluting than birth. In both cases the actions required to regain purity are prescribed and are scrupulously followed. The number of days the pollution is to last and the rituals to be performed each day vary according to caste. In addition, there are rules regarding one's diet and life-style during the period of pollution. Caste and line purity can only be regained if these rules are followed. One observes pollution rules only for *sātpuruṣ*, never for non-*bhāiyat* relatives. A married woman maintains a three-day pollution period at the death of her father or mother, but she does not observe death pollution for her brothers and sisters. The same married woman is, however, polluted by all deaths in her husband's *bhāiyat* (since it is now also her *bhāiyat*). Thus pollution can occur through either *gotra* or blood (*rakta*).

Members of a *baṇgśa* share *gotra* and *rakta*. Because incoming wives share the *gotra* of their husband's *bhāiyat* yet maintain the *rakta* of their father's, they offer water (*jal*) to the deceased in their father's as well as their husband's house. They offer water and food to the ancestors of their husbands once a year on the day when all ancestors are honored. Thus, the categories *bhāiyat, sātpuruṣ,* and *sapiṇḍa* (*piṇḍa* being the cooked rice the head of a house offers to the ancestors of the line) pertain to the same group in different contexts, the relatives included in the three groups being linked together in the same manner.

One's *bhāiyat* includes both close and more distant relatives linked to one through males (brothers and fathers) and through the marriages these males conclude (including the offspring of these marriages). All persons in one's *bhāiyat* are *jñati,* but the *jñati* is not a concrete group. One has *jñati* beyond the *bhāiyat,* and outside the *sātpuruṣ* group, in relationships so distant that the *gotra* label is the only reminder of a hypothetical and admittedly untraceable connection. Distant *jñati* need not observe death pollution, but because of shared *gotra,* they remain unavailable for marriage. But a line's daughter's daughter is sufficiently far removed to become eligible for marriage without infringing the blood rule.

Line, Blood, and the Bride

Marriage injunctions based on line and blood parallel indigenous delineations of persons and groups of persons. *Āttiya svajan* (*sva,* "self"; *jan,* "people"), the most general group of relatives, are "one's own people," the term *ātmā* referring to "self" rather than the "soul," which is most often used to translate the term. *Āttiya* is a general term meaning persons with whom one shares something in opposition to other groups of persons, *sharing, group,* and *person* being culturally defined. There are three groupings of *āttiya svajan.* First, one cannot marry persons with whom one shares blood and line, so one cannot marry *āttiya* with whom one shares blood and line. Hence blood and line are the exclusive bases of *āttiyata* (relatedness-to-self) defining the first grouping of relatives—*jñati,* or *rakta āttiya*—as opposed to the other two groupings. None of these grouping designations describes a group of people but rather, a category of relationship, even though *āttiya svajan* may suggest a concrete body of people because its designation entails both ego-based and non-ego-based constructs.

The second āttiya grouping designates relationships opposed to *jñati* relationships—that is, *kuṭum* relationships. *Kuṭum āttiya* are available for marriage, for they share only a code of conduct and selves constructed in similar ways through blood and marriage. The third *āttiya* grouping are "one's own" by relationship alone (*samparka*, or "link," via common code of conduct). If this relationship is sufficiently close (*nikaṭ*), then it too is enough to rule out the possibility of marriage; but in one sense or another all one's caste brothers are *āttiya*. Thus Bengalis say that one may marry someone with whom one already has a tie as long as this is not in the line (*baṇgśa*) or through blood (*rakta*) and as long as these *āttiya* are not *nijer* (own) or *nikaṭ* (near). The construction of the person through marriage, conception, birth, and blood provides the crucial distinction between those *āttiya* one can and cannot marry. (The full import of this assertion becomes clear in the last chapter.)

To summarize, the children of a couple share father's *rakta, baṇgśa, gotra, sapiṇḍa,* and *sātpuruṣ* (the boundaries of death pollution and ancestor worship). Despite the change in a married woman's *gotra* and *bhāiyat*, her father's 'line' of blood relatives are ineligible for marriage alliances with her husband's male line, the prohibition being extended to the husband's own *baṇgśa* and the woman's offspring.[4] The same injunction holds for a married woman's brothers' *baṇgśa*s. A female articulation of the relations among these *baṇgśa*s, both as a virgin and as a married woman, is significant. Although *baṇgśa*s are traced in the male line, they include women. But unlike men, who are born (and adopted) into a line, women are both born *and* married into lines. Hence, a distinction exists between daughters and wives of a line. Marriages are undertaken so that a man may start his own *baṇgśa* (*baṇgśa sthāpan karā*, to "establish a line" in much the same sense as deities are "installed" or "established" for worship).

Being born or being adopted into the line secures the continuation of lines through a combination of male and female in marriage. An adopted male can also continue the bloodline, so that both marriage and adoption concern the immortality of the line. Nevertheless there is a difference between having been born into a line and having been adopted into one, a distinction I leave for later.

The *Gotra* Question

In a sense, women are adopted as wives of the *baṇgśa* in exchange for the daughters of the *baṇgśa* who are adopted into other *baṇgśa* by a corresponding change of *gotra*. Persons of the same *gotra* cannot marry. *Gotra* is therefore a symbol shared by *āttiya* for expressing common *jñati* and *bhāiyat* ties within the larger *āttiya svajan* class. Thus shared *gotra* creates the opposition of *āttiya* to *kuṭum*. The *gotra* symbol also identifies one's *jñati* beyond the *sātpuruṣ* line. Although one can marry relatives outside the *sātpuruṣ*, one cannot marry those who have the same *gotra* as oneself, even if they are outside the *sātpuruṣ*.

*Gotra*s are titles or names persons hold and receive through their fathers. There are only a few major *gotra* names in each caste group. The lowest castes of Bengali *samāj*, however, do not have *gotra*s. Instead they have *thāk*s, geographical subgroupings that are (for purposes of marriage) the reverse of *gotra*. Thus each *thāk* is endogamous.[5] Among the lower castes, then, *baṇgśa* is the only unit into which one may not marry, whereas among the higher castes, the *gotra* rules for determining marriage ineligibility encompass a far larger number of *āttiya* than does *baṇgśa* alone. Hence, there may be closer marriages (among people already related) in lower than in higher *jāti*s.

*Gotra*s are said to have originated with the *ṛṣi*s (seers) in the ancient past. All those sharing *gotra* in a *jāti* are *jñati* to each other. Thus *gotra* is significant for marriage in that it is a symbol that distinguishes *jñati* from non-*jñati* (eligible from ineligible) without the necessity of tracing vertical lines of connection. Since *gotra* refers to synchronic relations, *rakta* is not equivalent to *gotra*, and as noted above, there may be a *rakta* tie among persons who do not share *gotra*. Thus *gotra* is not an inclusive category of the ineligible; yet shared *gotra* is enough to exclude a whole set of persons from consideration for marriage.

A *gotra* tie which signifies one's *jñati* obligates one to observe purity and pollution rules to a greater or lesser extent. This, however, raises the question: why does a woman who changes her *gotra* at marriage, observe birth and death pollution rules for her father's line? Like *kuṭum, āttiya, jñati,* and *baṇgśa* relationships, *rakta, gotra,* and *bhāiyat* relationships are all differentiated and articulated. Married women continue to share *rakta* with all their brothers and sisters but do not observe pollution rules at their deaths because they no longer share *baṇgśa, jñati,* and *sapiṇḍa*. Hence *rakta* is neatly distinguished from *gotra* and *bhāiyat*.

The change of *gotra* at marriage allows outsiders to become vehicles for the perpetuation of an ancestral male line. The incoming wives obey all the rules of purity and pollution of their husband's *jñati*. This is a complete change for a married woman, whose father's and mother's sides have nothing to do with her new *bhāiyat* and *paribār* (living persons of a household under a *kartā*, "head"). This is highlighted most effectively in the observance of death pollution.

Death pollution (*mṛttaśauc*) and obeying the impurity rules (*aśauc pālan karā*) relate directly to *gotra*. All members of a deceased person's *bhāiyat* and *baṇgśa* (daughters and wives included) go to the *ghāt* for purification during the *śrāddha* (mourning rites).[6] Beyond the *sātpuruṣ* these obligations are not strictly observed. *Jñati* outside the *sātpuruṣ* are distant (*dūr*) *āttiya*, and the expression "*ek diner jñati*" refers to *āttiya* whose death pollution is only observed, as a token, for one day. But even *ek diner jñati* are ineligible for marriage alliance.

Sampradān, the gift of a virgin, has to be made to persons not among *āttiya* encompassing *jñati*, *bhāiyat*, and *rakta āttiya* as separate categories of relatedness. *Jñati* cannot be turned into *kuṭum*, but the reverse is possible and is a preferred form of alliance. *Rakta* and *gotra* differentiate two subgroupings of *āttiya*, the *kuṭum* and the *jñati* of "one's own people." As stated in another context, "this would suggest that blood is male and while it is unchangeable, it is transmitted in the male line and is cut off at some point in the female line" (Fruzzetti and Östör, 1976b: 88).

Adoption and the Male Line

The process of adopting a male (*puruṣ*) to perpetuate one's line contrasts with what happens to a female in marriage. Marriage (*biye*) is a form of adoption in that women pass from one *baṇgśa* to another. Both marriage and adoption serve the same purposes: the continuation of a line and the fulfullment of *dharma*.[7] Similar *mantras* are recited both in adoption and at marriage when the groom accepts (*grahaṇ karā*) the gift of a virgin, publicly transforming her into a wife. Male adoption highlights the ambiguous position of women in Bengali marriage. The ambiguity stems from the positioning of a married woman between two *baṇgśa*s and houses as daughter of the one and wife of the other.

A man without issue (*santān*) can adopt his daughter's son (*dahittra putra*, 'son-through-a-daughter') to perpetuate his line. Manu calls a woman *svavasinī*, a "dweller with her own people," in a relationship to her father that is not severed after marriage. According to Manu, a father can make his daughter into a *putrikā* (female for *putra*, "son") by reciting a formula: "the male child born of her shall perform my funeral rites."[8] Furthermore, "as a son, so does the daughter of a man proceed from his several limbs. How then should any other person take her father's wealth?"[9]

In the adoption of a daughter's son the *nāti* (DS) changes *gotra* from that of his father to that of his mother's father, even though his mother has at marriage changed her *gotra* from that of her father to that of her husband. By changing his *gotra* to that of his mother's father (*dādu*), a boy will be able to continue his *dādu*'s *baṇgśa*. The nature of the transformation is crucial: the daughter's son does not undergo a transubstantiation of blood; his blood remains that of his father just as a woman's remains that of her father after marriage. In both cases the indigenous construction of blood and line is the key to the transformation. Women do not transmit the blood of their fathers, even though both mother and father contribute to the blood of the child. Blood, itself male, is transmitted in the male line alone. Yet a daughter's son is, nonetheless, suitable for adoption because the mother's blood that complements the father's blood in conception (as I explain in the last section of this chapter) is in fact the blood of a *male* line, the mother's father's blood. The male blood tie between *dādu* (MF) and *nāti* (DS) is indisputable. In the adoption ceremony, only the *gotra* and the *baṇgśa*'s purity and impurity rules are emphasized, the significant change being (as in the case of marriage) the change of *gotra*.

The difference between marriage and adoption is what happens to blood: in male adoption, a prior blood tie is preferred, whereas in female marriage, there cannot be a trace of prior blood connection. The similarity between adopted boys and married women is that both change *gotra*s: both adopted sons and married women obey the death pollution rules of their *own* mothers and fathers. Similarly, an adopted son observes the full death pollution period of his new father's *jñati* just as a married woman obeys the pollution rules of her father-in-law's *jñati*.[10] Thus, the *baṇgśa* is constructed out of birth, marriage, or adoption, each being indigenously understood, each being reciprocally linked with different classes of *āttiya*.

Persons of an ancestor's line are born into the line. They all share *gotra* and *rakta*, male to male, which is only made possible by bringing in women with different *gotra* and different *rakta*, and by transforming the *gotra*s of these women through marriage. Being of different blood, the women can transmit the male line. The marriage relations (*kuṭum*) are transformed into *jñati* (*gotra*) and blood relations from the vantage point of the succeeding generation. In this way the FB (*kākā*), FBW (*kākīmā*), B, BS, FF, and SS as well as unmarried sisters, BW, BSW, and SW are one's *bhāiyat*. Some of these are relatives by blood (*rakta*), others by marriage, yet all are *bhāiyat*. By contrast, one's own *kuṭum*—WB, WF-M, ZHB—are neither *jñati* nor relatives by blood. Furthermore, married sisters and FZ and MZ are relatives by blood though neither of one's *bhāiyat* nor of one's *jñati.* Thus, *baṇgśa, gotra, rakta,* and marriage are cultural categories which enter into complex relationships in the indigenous construction of the person. Marriage rules and *rakta, baṇgśa,* and *gotra* rules in the definition of persons as classes of relatives are linked to the rules of hierarchy (the principles of pure and impure) in caste society.

Male and Female: Marriage, Conception, Birth, and the Person

Rakta, gotra, baṇgśa are different categories, but they are all transmitted from male to male through women. *Baṇgśa* is perpetuated through the passage of male blood. The importance of blood is its passage from male to male through females. Blood transmission is made possible by the wives' being a receptacle and a transmitter.

Women, then, are the only means through which a man can continue his line and transmit his ancestral male blood. It is the indigenous construction of blood that links him to previous and succeeding generations of males: F, FF and FS, SS. This immortality of the line is made possible by the birth of male children through a wife (*strī, bou*). Brides (*patris*) are regarded as vessels and grooms (*patras*) as the ones who install or contain the vessels. The terms for installing and establishing are *sthāpan karā* and *pratiśṭhā karā* (also used in connection with the consecration of a deity's clay image). The installation of a line (*baṇgśa*) has the same meaning: giving life to a line by creating an issue (*santān*) through women. This inversion of the relation between gods and men—humanizing the gods and deifying the line—is, as I have said, much favored by Hindu ideologies. Lines have deities (the *kuladebātās*) whose worship is established and continued by males from father to son. The installations of a deity and of a line in marriage are parallel and related acts, both being performed by Brāhmaṇ priests amidst sacred ritual.

The vessel and the holder of the vessel reflect a relationship between an all-encompassing and an all-encompassed unit.[11] "The most common reference to marriage is in terms of a field and the seed in the field. Woman is the field (*khettra*), the cultivator provides the seed and 'cultures' the field" (Fruzzetti and Östör, 1976b: 96). Men are the owners (*mālik*) of the field and they cultivate (*cās karā*) the earth. Women view themselves as the field which men plough and farm. The world (*prithibi*) and the earth are female. Like Sitā—who is born of the earth and goes back to the earth—women regard themselves as mother earth. Earth receives the seeds of men and gives back the fruit (*phol*) of men: children, both male and female. Mother earth herself receives 'femaleness,' the placenta (also called *phol*), which is buried in the earth by the midwife. The placenta is a woman's accumulated 10 months and 10 days of menstrual blood and is culturally conceived as a female (*meyeder*) thing (*jinis*). It remains in and is a part of the earth. It is *prithibir paona* (world's gift).[12] Male blood continues the male line through children, whereas femaleness maintains ties with and replenishes mother earth. In women's rituals, the symbols of the earth are always tied to the concept of "femaleness," *mātṛ śakti* (women's divine or sacred power), and female sexuality. Similarly, *khettra* is used to refer to one's children.

Husband and wife (*swāmī strī*) are the seed and field, the former sowing the *bīj* (seed), the latter bearing the *phol*. In time the fruit ripens and falls, breaking the 36 *nāṛis* (navels, or umbilical cords) that connect mother and child. The child belongs to the father's line, and the mother's line sustains the earth. Like the field and vessel, women receive and accept (*grahaṇ karā*) the seed of their husbands. Women "house" the seed in their wombs; the womb contains the male *baṇgśa*. The seed, the male element (*puruṣ*), is here encompassed by the womb, the vessel, which is also the female element (*śakti, prakriti*). Before birth, femaleness encompasses maleness; after birth maleness encompasses femaleness in the male line.

Seed is produced in the bone marrow (*majja*) of men and builds the bones of the child. It becomes blood in the womb (*garbha*). Mothers nourish (*lālan pālan karā*) and augment the male blood as the child grows. After birth, the mother continues to nourish the child through her milk.

The birth of a child comes about "through the father" (*bābā diye janma*), but it is given by the mother (*janma dātā*, "giver of birth"). "*Rakta* thus is a substance which is conceptualized in Bengali terms as having issued from the seed, the carrier of the father's *baṇgśa dhārā* (line) and *gotra*, complemented and nourished in and through the mother, both blood and affect" (Fruzzetti and Östör, 1976a: 99). The complementarity of maleness/femaleness (*puruṣ/prakriti*) parallels earth/seed, encompasser of the *baṇgśa* and encompassed by the *baṇgśa;* and all these parallels emphasize that male is not opposed to female. Therefore, mother complements the father in every step of the creation of a child.

"All human beings (*mānuṣ*) share the female and male qualities, with the difference that women (*strī lok, nāṛi jāti*) have the former, men (*puruṣ*), the latter, in greater proportion. This complementarity is noticeable on every level" (Fruzzetti and Östör, 1976b: 98). The mother's thing (*māyer jinis*) or quality (*gūṇ*) together with the father's quality (*puruṣ gūṇ*) determines the child's sex. Through blood and milk, the mother strengthens the child's bone and increases his flesh and blood. In the world of men, the father cares for and tends to the child and looks after his intelligence (*buddhī,* a male quality), while the mother prepares and makes the child competent for the *saṇgsār* (daily household activities) and for the role of householder in the *saṇgsār.*

The child is conceived (born of) and introduced (*paricay*) to the world by the father. Females—mothers—cannot "introduce" children to the world, that being the right (*adhikār*) of males. Women are givers of "birth," but men introduce the issue of the line to their ancestors and to the world of living. *Paricay* refers to the physical, social, and intellectual introduction of the child to all things and beings around him. A man's origin and relationship to the ancestors are his *paricay. Paricay* is the same for male and female children, but it is for males that *paricay* is crucial since they carry the line. Names of both daughters and sons are kept in the *baṇgśa talika,* the list of ancestors and lines, for two reasons: first, so that all children know their ancestors; second, so that lines can be matched in marriage negotiations (especially important for a daughter).

The conception and birth of a child as locally understood relates to the transformation of women through marriage. Women leave their own *baṇgśa* on marriage. The married woman receives her *paricay* through a male, in this case her husband; and the fruit of the marriage—the children—receive their *paricay* through the same man. Children acquire all the categories of *āttiya* through birth (*bhāiyat, jñati,* and *sātpuruṣ,* some of whom are *kuṭum* to their parents); a woman, however, acquires *āttiya* through marriage and a change of *gotra.* The difference between the two stems from the difference of construction between daughters of a line and wives of a line.

Children cannot be given in marriage to their mother's brother's line (which is their own MB *baṇgśa*) or to the line into which the MZ (*māsī*) is married. All these people share blood. Children of sisters cannot marry even though their lines, *gotras,* and houses are of necessity different (unless two brothers have married two sisters), for sisters share their father's blood. Thus, the union of MZS-MZD would amount to a breach of the blood rule even though it conformed to the *gotra* and *baṇgśa* rules. Shared blood also implies continued observation of pollution rules, so that even after marriage a married woman's father and brother must perform certain acts at the death rituals of persons belonging to her new *jñati.*

The woman's "quality" and "thing," her femaleness (*mātṛ śakti*), is shared by her sons and daughters; hence daughters of the line cannot be carriers of the line. Having the same *mātṛ śakti* as her husband would make it impossible for a woman to give life to the seed. *Mātṛ śakti* is given to a man so that a *baṇgśa* may be started. Men are born into lines, and *mātṛ śakti* has to be given to a line to perpetuate it. This is why women must leave the *gotra* and *baṇgśa* they are born into and enter into a new *gotra* and *baṇgśa,* creating the in-between, temporary position of women within the system of lines and castes. A man's place is fixed in the line and *gotra,* but women come into and go out of lines. The three generations of females in a household are all outsiders, all having come from different lines, different *gotras*. In summary, it can be said that "the whole ideology and symbolism of marriage and birth is designed . . . to express, interpret and define the coming and going of women between *baṇgśa*s . . . [as well as] the meaning of being male and female" (Fruzzetti and Östör, 1976a: 102).

As I have shown in the previous section, blood relationships exist even where there is no *gotra, jñati,* and *baṇgśa* connection. Marriage links lines by the giving and accepting of a virgin in marriage. The marriage rules governing *gotra, rakta,* and *baṇgśa* relatedness have to be observed before an alliance can be concluded, lest the line be destroyed by inability of husband and wife to give new life. Lines cannot be perpetuated unless the difference of *rakta* and *mātṛ śakti* between bride and groom can be maintained.[13] On the mother's side, blood connection is considered to disappear within three generations; on the father's side it remains up to seven generations and beyond.

The three major rules for marriage may be stated briefly: first, the avoidance of close relatives (*āttiya* with whom one shares blood or *mātṛ śakti* or both); second, the avoidance of shared *gotra;* third, the avoidance of the houses and lines into which a MZ was married. "Bad blood" requires the third rule; the girl or her MZ might meet with death, incurable disease, or other calamity in her MZ's in-laws' house (*śvaśur bāṛi*), whereas a girl may be given to her FZ's *śvaśur bāṛi.* The marriage of a girl into her MZ's *ghar* would pose problems at the *ghāt* when the death rituals are performed. A girl and her MZ cannot "sit at the same *ghāt,*" since someone from the MB's or B's house has to go to the *ghāt* to "lift" a married daughter or sister from death pollution. This expresses a blood relation since the same *ghāt* which a girl would share with her MZ as *jñati* would also include the girl's father or brother and her MZ's brother or father (who are also her *māmā* and *dādu*), thus reversing the roles of wife-givers and wife-takers in death rituals.

Women, then, are merely the receptacles and transmitters, never the carriers, of a line. The coming to and going from *baṇgśas* by women; the male dominance in the "line"; the male/female complementary categories of persons and groups of persons whereby women "belong" to a line as daughters because of birth but are "in" but not "of" a line after marriage—all seem to indicate the ambiguous position of women. In fact, there is no such ambiguity. The meaning and symbolism of *sampradān* is in what the gift accomplishes: the creation and continuation of the line, the joining of lines *through* women, the attainment of immortality for one's own line. The gift, furthermore, maintains caste status and purity as well as equivalence and unity, for the gift of a virgin may only be given to caste brothers. Having considered the major marriage rules, the father of the virgin (through the ritual of marriage) makes the offer of his daughter to the groom. The offer (*dān*) is witnessed by men, gods and ancestors, relatives, friends, caste brothers, *kuṭum,* and *jñati*—all of whom bless the union. Marriage itself being a sacred sacrament among Hindus, the central symbol of gifting a virgin guarantees the immortality of men through their lines. Thus men "give" to receive, and women are exchanged to tie men to each other through the line, maintaining *purity* and *jāti* equivalence and also creating the differences necessary for the conclusion of future alliances.

CHAPTER 2

Pon:
Ritual and the Meaning of Prestations

Dowry, Status, and Power in the Household in Relation to the Sacred Gift

Women, Dowry, and Ritual

The sociological significance of dowry payments is directly related to the position of women in Hindu society. The purity of a *baṇgśa* in a *ghar* is, in turn, tied to the purity of women.[1] Women, as wives, can continue and maintain a male line, but they can also destroy a line through misbehavior. Immoral (or other) actions that go against the conduct appropriate to women's lines of birth or marriage jeopardize the purity and therefore the status of those lines. Since women of one's own *baṇgśa* cannot maintain the lines of their fathers and brothers, they must be given away so that their natal *baṇgśa* can receive other women, the exchange itself serving the same basic purpose of continuing the line.

The payment of dowry (*pon*) accompanies the gift (*dān*) of a virgin. Although both gifts are symbolized in the marriage ritual, they must be differentiated to clarify the meaning of each in relation to the conceptualization of women as daughters and as wives of a line, and in relation to the difference between status and power.[2] In Hindu marriage the dowry is quite separate from the gift of a virgin (*sam-*

pradān). Nevertheless, the two transactions are related and together express a Bengali version of marriage alliance (*ādān pradān*). Furthermore, the patterns of gift giving and prestations accompanying the various stages of the ritual trace the ideological implications of giving, receiving, and the roles involving women in the various kinds of exchange.

Gifts mark a marriage link between two groups and establish the possibility of further ties. Dowry is one of these gifts, but the giving of dowry itself is a composite exchange with distinct portions going to the groom, the groom's father, the bride, and the couple as a unit. The gifts themselves are hierarchized in terms of sacred (pure and impure) status, political influence, and economic power. Dowry (*pon*), rewards for functional caste duties (*paona*s), and gifts in the *jajmani* system (*dābi*s) parallel ideology and action in the hierarchical society. The gift of a virgin and the economic role of dowry express principles basic to Bengali society, and it is the separation as well as the link between status and power that yield hierarchy and give a crucial place to women in society. The sacred nature and economic power of marriage are brought together and infused with meaning through the ritual's performance.

Marriages do not just occur. First, it must be made certain that the prospective partners are not of the same *gotra* and, second, that there is no *rakta* connection on the mother's side to the third degree.[3] Thus the nature of the first gift, the bride, is important and is negotiated separately from (though with a direct influence on) the dowry. The dowry in turn may dictate the final decision on the acceptance of the first gift. This does not mean that a wealthy *ghar* can contravene caste and kinship principles, that a poorer house would consent to giving a daughter to a wealthier but lower status *ghar,* or that a wealthy house can infringe the blood role to keep its wealth in the house. Rather, the general marriage rules serve to direct and limit the range of possible unions in terms of categories of persons available for marriage.

When the offering of a virgin in marriage is considered, the giver bears in mind that the receivers will demand a second gift if they consent to the first (the virgin). There is a difference in the nature of the two exchanges: the first is a sacred gift, the highest possible, and can be neither argued about nor contested, whereas the second gift (*pon*) is a *dābi,* a demand rightfully made by the groom in return for accepting the bride. A girl's father has both gifts in mind when he starts looking for a groom. Both dowry and bride represent wealth, but the children to be born after marriage are the true wealth of a line and house. This leads to a question: if the gift of the virgin is the highest form of giving, then why does the dowry play such an important role in accepting or rejecting the girl? The answer is found in the attitude toward women in Bengali *samāj* (society).

It is believed that daughters should be married and not kept in their father's house for too long. Since a woman has to be a mother before she can become a complete person, the foremost duty of a father is to find husbands for his daughters. The presence of unmarried women is inauspicious for the men of the house and taints the *ghar* in the eyes of those who have disposed of their daughters and who may be willing to take women for their sons. The mere presence of marriageable women is impure for a house; the fear of incest is strong. In contrast, the acceptance of these women by lines with whom neither *gotra* nor *rakta* is shared is auspicious and bountiful. Inmarrying women are deities of the house, continuing and increasing the male lines.

The purity of one's women has to be maintained, and the best way to ensure this is by giving them away in time. Unmarried women express and reflect the status and prestige of their line and house to those looking for brides. Thus women have to be married into good houses and lines. The same pressure is not experienced in relation to sons since sons are not the guardians of purity. A daughter is rarely given to a line that does not demand dowry, for the size of the dowry reflects the prestige and honor of the line accepting the gift of the virgin.[4] On the other hand, the possibility of having one's women refused is recognized and feared because rejection decreases the prestige of bride-givers.

Daughters are clearly distinguished from wives of a line. The former must be given to other lines; the latter must be brought into one's own line. Just as the children of an unmarried woman destroy her father's line, so too the children of a wife ensure the immortality of her husband's line. Here is the duality of women's nature—auspicious and inauspicious, creative and destructive—which women share with the gods in Bengali cosmogony. Hence elaborate rituals surround the gift of a virgin and seemingly unbalance the economics of dowry giving. Bride-givers give unilaterally, expecting nothing concrete in return.[5] The inequality of givers and receivers is established by the gift itself (the *kanyā*, or "virgin") and by the ritual which brings the two groups of people together through the marriage alliance. But this inequality does not adhere permanently to these groups as givers and receivers in relation to other lives. Rather, it refers to their position in the ritual itself.

Marriage Negotiations

Marriage negotiations are always initiated by the father or guardian of a marriageable girl, though the father of an unmarried boy may announce to his *jñati* and *kuṭum* that his son is ready for marriage. A girl's father also may put out the news that his daughter is available for marriage. The local expression for a woman's readiness is *phul phutece* ("the blossom has ripened or opened"). Information is passed on even by houses with no potential marriage partners, for in time they will themselves need information from others. But it is the girl's father who will proceed on the basis of such news. He might use the suggestions of relatives (*āttiya*), especially near ones (*nikaṭ āttiya*). He might also actively look for a groom among the *kuṭum* (more than likely in the houses of his sister-in-law's father and his daughter's husband, who may have available grooms among *their* relatives by marriage). A SWB or a DHB are ideal choices. A guardian may hire a professional go-between (*ghatak*) to find brides or grooms for a house and to supply all the information necessary for a girl's father to initiate the formal negotiations. The heads of the respective households need not even meet while negotiating the dowry, only getting together to finalize the deal. With this, the *ghatak*'s services terminate; he acts merely as a messenger. Fathers of marriageable girls can also call on the services of their caste brothers (*jāti bhāis*). In cities, matrimonial advertising in newspapers serves the same purpose.

Initiating an inquiry with a particular *ghar* does not mean that the girl's guardian is obligated to follow through or even notify the *ghar* of his intentions. It is, however, necessary to get a favorable answer to the inquiry from the prospective groom's house before a second step can even be considered. Once negotiations are in full motion and there is enough interest on both sides, questions are asked about the dowry. But before any details can be discussed, the bride herself must pass some tests: her appearance must be pleasing, her height proper, her complexion pale, and her bearing good—so a photograph is sent to the groom's house once the latter responds to the initial contact. The bride's educational level, experience, and accomplishments are also taken into consideration. Most important, her horoscope (*koṣṭhi bicār*) must be examined. The horoscope tells whether the couple is compatible, whether their characters, fates, planets, and futures are in harmony.

Once the guardians meet to discuss the dowry, the questions of appearance and qualifications are no longer discussed. The future groom is not present at these talks since he must maintain a *bhadra* (proper, genteel, respectful) relationship with his future father-in-law. First, the expectations of the groom's household are clearly stated regardless of the high or low *bhadra* status of either house. Second, the specifics of the dowry are stated—how much of it should be in cash, in goods (e.g., jewelry, household items), or in other property. The groom's side will put the case for a higher dowry than they really expect to get. They will agree to lower their demands as the negotiations go on, but such a lowering lessens the respect and status of the bride's side. Haggling over the dowry proceeds much the same way as haggling over goods and services in the bazaar.

If the dowry is too high or if the girl's guardian does not like the people in the groom's house, he can withdraw his offer of alliance. If the house of the potential husband has too many unmarried children, the resources of the bride-givers would be drained, since they are expected to make gifts at all marriages of the *ghar.* Too many children also mean more work for a young bride in the house. The groom's side can also terminate negotiations at this stage if they aren't satisfied with the dowry offered or if they are not given proper respect. Negotiations can be terminated within a few days or can be carried on for months or years in cases where the stakes are high.

It is the couple's *bhāgga* (good fortune or luck) that determines whether the negotiations are fruitful. Some marriages are negotiated in days, and the rituals are completed within a few weeks (10 days altogether in one case I witnessed in Vishnupur) once the astrologically auspicious time is set for the performance. In cases where the marriage negotiations are called off, the girl's side begins to look for a new groom. Most often, the question of the dowry is the cause for terminating negotiations, but wealth itself is not the criterion of status. A house may prefer to give a daughter to a high-status but less wealthy house. In these cases the dowry reflects the prestige of the givers. The reverse may be equally true of dowries given by less wealthy high-status houses. Hence hierarchy and caste status are central factors in negotiations. Lines and houses within a caste have variable status despite their membership in the same caste, since intracaste equality is only reflected outward, in relation to another caste. The guardian has one aim in mind: to marry off all of his unmarried daughters and to marry them well. In this sense he must abide by caste and kinship rules, the rules of the *samāj.* To give one's own women to houses with whom one shares either *rakta* or *gotra* would breach norms and regulations of the *samāj,* in which case *ghar* members could suffer outcasting or exclusion from their own *bhāiyat.* The purity of women is maintained by adhering to the marriage rules, and this in turn affects the purity of the *ghar* which gives the bride.

The Alliance System in Bengal

Ādān pradān is the Bengali system of marriage alliance whereby women and prestations are, according to certain principles, passed from one category of people to another.[6] Marriages establish lines of blood and link these lines to each other, with the arrangements for determining the ties among many segmentary lines referred to as *ādān pradān*. Since *ādān pradān* creates units of equivalence within the larger unity of the *jāti*, *baṇgśa*s have to be matched to each other before a marriage can take place. The statuses of the contracting lines and houses should be as close as possible. Marriage alliance in Bengal establishes the equivalence of different lines and houses. *Baṇgśa*s, or lines, are the smallest units of equivalence; the units created by marriage are *kula*s and *baṇgśa*s (farther or closer points of segmentation on a line), *ghar*s and *paribār*s (households in the narrower and wider sense), with the notion of the line encompassing, or hierarchically dominant over, the notion of the locality (household) (Fruzzetti, Östör, and Barnett, 1976).

Ādān pradān, then, is the language of alliance in Bengal; it relates to the giving and taking of women among lines and to the passage of prestations. These extend through generations in some cases and terminate with a single marriage in others. In the Bengali alliance system there are no actual, fixed groups to whom one has to keep giving women or from whom one has to keep taking women; nor is there any fixed pattern of exchanging women in terms of the direction or frequency of marriages. In other words, the Bengali system does not follow the classical pattern of hypergamy.[7] The reversal of the direction of marriage is quite common in Bengal. Such unions are known as *badal biye* (exchange marriage), and these are as common as marriages in entirely new directions. The absence of fixed groups of exchange does not imply intercaste marriages but does suggest that castes cannot be broken down into groups of bride-givers or bride-takers. In Bengali marriages, lines are matched in terms of status as well as power. *Ādān pradān* emphasizes the line and the nature of the lines involved. It forms the core concern of marriage negotiations.

Negotiating a marriage alliance is difficult, and the process may be damaging to the lines involved. Marrying within the circle of one's *kuṭum* may be a blessing or a misfortune. Of the many *kuṭum* negotiations I attended, four terminated before completion. The main reason given was the amount of dowry: marriages involving *kuṭum ghar* are attended by high dowry demands. It is preferable to give a daughter to a *ghar* where one is already known, where there are some of one's own women, or where one has taken women from before. Because of this the dowry is set high—the givers want to continue a previous relationship.

The groom's side knows how much dowry the bride's father can afford. Paying a high dowry for one's daughter attracts other well placed lines and *ghar*s into the alliance circle as both givers and receivers. Status, prestige, and reputation are in this way enhanced. A high dowry is also a sign of *bhadra* (respected) households. The absence of haggling over dowry shows concern and respect for the future and security of one's daughters. Daughters of such houses are much sought after.

If negotiations are broken off and a girl is refused, her chances for a good alliance decrease. Other houses will demand a higher dowry, citing the previous refusal as justification. A groom's desirability likewise decreases if he is refused because of personality reasons, for demanding too high a dowry, or for taking too long to make a decision; these are the types of *ghar*s avoided by the guardians of unmarried women. Nevertheless, the groom's side has the upper hand. As I have said, the question of property is also crucial, and considerations such as looks, education, and age (of the girl) may be outweighed by an unusually high dowry.[8] Discussions about the dowry take place in private. The dowry itself is given in the presence of witnesses (one hears of cases where the payment was later denied), and the gift of the virgin is made through the priest with relatives, ancestors, and deities for witnesses.

Other factors influencing the alliance between two lines are the social, political, and economic conditions (*samājik* and *arthanaitik abostha*) of the houses involved. The standing of the *ghar* refers to relative prestige, status, wealth, and living conditions. It is important to know how the *ghar* is regarded in the locality (and among its caste fellows in other places), where they have established previous marriages, and whether they have *bhadra* contacts. There are a number of other questions to consider carefully before negotiating a dowry: does the *ghar,* giving or taking the virgin, own land; is it an old, established line; is it living in the ancestral house; and what kind of business does it have?[9] The higher a dowry one is prepared to pay, the more critical one is of the bride-takers' house. If the bride's *ghar* are landowners, they prefer to give a daughter to people who also own land, even if the groom has separate employment. Similarly, the groom's side would prefer their *kuṭum* to own land. A bride's father who has independent income (e.g., a lawyer, doctor, or merchant) is now considered just as good as a landowner.

The next question asked is the groom's profession. The girl's family want to know his income and employment in government or private enterprise. Government employment is preferred since those jobs are permanent. The bride's employment is not questioned since she is not expected to have a job; she is judged by her fathers' and brothers' positions. Today, however, her education is considered important. A college girl—especially one with a postgraduate degree—is more desirable than a girl with no education. Brides are, in addition, expected to sing, sew, and cook. The bride should be talented in the arts, clever, and capable of running the *saṇgsār*. Being fair-complexioned with long, jet-black hair, and slender (neither too fat nor too thin since both are a sign of disease) are desirable in a girl. She should be soft-spoken, gentle, and soft-skinned, with dove-like eyes in the image of the Goddesses Durgā or Lakṣmī (reflecting the complexion and beauty of a deity). Few girls satisfy all of the above requirements, but at least one or two ideals of beauty are desired in a bride.

Desirable male characteristics are somewhat different. Although one prefers a fair-complexioned groom without physical defects, these are not the attributes by which a groom is judged. The bride's side wants to know if he has a steady income, if he is a heavy smoker or drinker, and if he associates with women of ill-repute or other antisocial groups. This type of information can easily be obtained from the *ghatak* or one's *kuṭum* and friends. A man with too many vices will not tend to the *saṇgsār*; this will ruin the happiness of a married daughter.

It is not easy either to give away a daughter or to acquire a wife for one's son (an ill-tempered bride can destroy a *ghar* and its people within months), so hesitation at facing a "total stranger" is shared by both houses. Parents prefer giving a daughter to a known *ghar* or at least to a place where one has acquaintances or *kuṭum.* Preferably, daughters should go to a nearby place. There are some cases of Vishnupuri marriages with high-standing houses as far away as Delhi, Bombay, and America, but there are other cases in which marriage did not take place because of the distance of the house and hesitation on the bride's side. Once an alliance is formed with a particular *ghar* it is meant to continue. This is done in part by visitations back and forth, attending each other's festivals and marriages. A married daughter is expected to visit her father's house as often as possible.

There is, then, a preference on the part of townspeople to give daughters to or take brides from the same area. With a few exceptions, the marriages I attended during three years of fieldwork were contracted with *ghar*s within a radius of 30 miles or less.[10] The choice of an area within which one gives or takes women varies according to the *ghar*. One of the Poddar (goldsmith caste) *ghar*s prefers women within the town, from a group to whom they have given or from whom they have taken women in the past. This pattern of marriage preferences for either a bride or groom is consistent with both Muslim and Hindu practices. Another possibility is to limit one's choice of a bride or groom to a single locality (village or town) by taking brides from, for example, Burdwan district, Bankura town, or a village in Midnapur district. This is one way of strengthening the marriage tie with one's *kuṭum* or the *kuṭum* of *kuṭum*: the journey one makes to a married daughter's house is also a visit to relatives. Marriages are not an end in themselves; the postmarital visitations (*āsājaoyā*, going back and forth between each other's houses) and prestations are the very essence of marriage alliances.

One does not begin an alliance with a house by giving a daughter and end the exchange with the completion of the marriage rituals. Thus townspeople who left their ancestral home to settle in Calcutta still come back to marry women from Vishnupur. "Home" marriages help one maintain ties with one's own people left in town. In the cases where young men come home to marry from far away places, the dowries are set lower to counteract the unwillingness of the bride's side to give women to distant houses. On the other hand, there are townspeople who like to give their daughters to lines and houses with whom they have had no previous exchanges. In these cases, the bride-givers have (for one reason or another) severed all relations with their *jñati* and *kuṭum* and desire to initiate an entirely new set of alliances.

When alliances are concluded the (seemingly) locality-based units of *ghar* and *paribār* are fully encompassed within the *baṇgśa* and *kula*, the segmentary units of male lines. The concept of line cuts across *jñati* (blood-relative) and *kuṭum* (marriage-relative) formations. Since some *kuṭum* are eligible for further alliances with one's own *baṇgśa*, their lines will have to be matched to one's own.[11] Previous marriages therefore play a part in considering future marriages.

The purity or impurity of a line reflects on the other lines linked to it by marriage and affects the minimal as well as the maximal units: the couple contracting the marriage, the line issuing from their children, the whole marriage circle, and eventually the entire endogamous subcaste. If, in the past, women were given to lower (*nicu*) status lines, the lowness of the wife-takers reflects on the status of the givers. Furthermore, any impure actions committed by persons in one's *bhāiyat* affect the status of the whole male line. A line has to maintain a code of conduct. If a single member of the *bhāiyat* seriously infringed a caste or kinship rule three or four generations back, the present group of the same line has to bear the consequences.

In matching lines for marriage, the lines' codes as well as the *jāti*'s codes for conduct are considered. People want to know if the lines involved have interdined with higher status or lower status groups, if the lines have interdined and participated in each others' festivals in the past, if they have been guests at each others' marriage and funeral feasts, if they have contracted intercaste marriages, and if they have accumulated bad wealth. Thus the unit of equivalence is stated anew with each marriage: status, purity, and equivalence in these terms have to be recalculated each time as they affect the larger units of equivalence and thus the statuses of other lines. Each new marriage brings new criteria into the alliance system of *ādān pradān*. As more and more lines are brought into the circle, the opportunity to continue or repeat previous alliances becomes greater. On the other hand, each new marriage may change the system enough to start an entirely new direction for future exchanges. The questions of status and power are not contradictory. The considerations of status are the context within which other factors may decide the actual choice: "Alliance depends on two constructions of difference—difference among hierarchical units, which operates through their separation, and a difference within units of equivalence which operates through exchange and combination" (Fruzzetti, Östör, and Barnett, 1976: 183). In Bengali *ādān pradān*, each particular alliance determines these units.

The Economics of the Dowry

Pon (dowry) is by its nature physical and changeable, increased or decreased according to the desirability of an alliance. Although dowry is a mere contract, the gift of the virgin is unalterable and sacred. This is the difference between *dābi* (demand, due) and *dān* (a gift freely bestowed). After marriage the bride's contact with her father's house lessens, and she becomes the economic liability of her in-laws. This responsibility is considered a burden, one which should be shared by the bride's father. Thus the dowry initiates a series of other smaller gifts from the bride's father's house to that of the in-laws, a pattern which is carried on by the bride's brothers after her father's death.

Dān: the items offered as dowry goods.

The gift of the virgin is dictated by caste and kinship principles, whereas the dowry is dictated by the sheer availability of cash and property. The two cannot be equated and the criteria for one cannot be reduced to those for the other. The virgin is given amidst the rites of *kanyā dān*; the dowry is paid before the marriage.

The amount of dowry paid fluctuates greatly according to the economic condition, as opposed to the caste status, of a household. Dowries range between Rs.100,000 (paid by the wealthiest business and landowning houses in the town) and Rs.10 or less (paid by the poorest sweepers). The majority of the lowest placed economic groups give a pair of earrings, a *sāri*, a few utensils, and some cash. Most sections of the community are burdened by dowry demands higher than they can afford. One woman I spoke with had been saving up since 1967 for a bicycle to give to her future son-in-law. The marriage was performed in 1973, and even then the bicycle was the only dowry item.

The dowry is never given in cash alone, even though the groom's side attempts to get as much of it in cash as possible. Land can be given as part of the dowry if the bride has no brothers and would thus inherit the property (*sampatti*) anyway. The marriage settlement will also specify the installments in which the dowry is to be given, with one-half or one-third given in cash to the groom and his family a few days or weeks before the marriage is made final. The remainder is divided into several parts, with one part being spent on jewelry for the bride, the type of ornament and the jeweler being specified. The groom's side can request receipts for the ornaments to verify that the right amount was spent on the right quality jewelry. The groom's *ghar* might ask for items such as a motorcycle, refrigerator, or car as part of the original dowry.

There are other items the guardian of the bride might give his daughter. These goods are a part of the father's *dān* to his daughter, not a part of the marriage *pon.* Fathers offer *dān* to their married daughters. These are gifts which accompany her to her in-laws' house. These gifts are freely given without any demands being made by the groom and bride. The cash and other requested items are part of the joint property the bride shares with the rest of the husband's *ghar,* whereas the jewelry and clothing the bride receives are her own private possessions. The rest of the *dān* (kitchen utensils, clothes) is normally shared by the *ghar* as a whole unless the newly married couple take up separate residence.

The cash part of the *pon* is divided into several parts, one of which is used to purchase the first set of prestations the groom's house must send to the bride on the day of the *gāe halud tattva* (turmeric-smearing ritual—*tattva* means "expected gifts"). The rest might go into paying for all or part of the feast the groom's *ghar* gives for relatives and friends on the fourth day after the marriage. This is *bou bhāt* ('wife-rice'), when the bride is fully accepted into her husband's own *samāj* and *jāti* (society and caste). Accepting cooked food from her means that her new relatives regard her as a member of their *ghar,* that she is accepted as an equal into the local *jāti* group.

Though groom and *kanyā* never take part in the negotiations (that being *abhādra,* "not respectable"), the groom does express his wishes before the actual negotiations. A settlement is never concluded straight away; enough time is given to the groom to consider the offer and decide accordingly. Once the actual working of the *pon* contract is settled, the future father-in-law offers the groom a special gift such as a bicycle, a watch, a golden chain, or a ring.

Many other gifts and exchanges accompany the long and detailed marriage ceremonies, but I do not take these up here since they belong more properly to a discussion of the rituals during which the gifts are exchanged.

The Significance and Meaning of Gift Giving

Gifts and Relatives

Ceremonial gift giving is a feature of birth, marriage, and death rituals in Bengal. Gift and ritual are linked together; the giving is understood in relation to the rites in which the gifts are made. The gift of a virgin elicits a series of gift exchanges before, during, and after the performance of marriage. *Sampradān,* the gift of the virgin, is a bestowal, one which is made through the mediation of a priest with all the gods and ancestors for witnesses. This is a sacred gift (not a *paona* or a *dābi*), freely rendered and meaningful only in the ritual's context. It is not made in return for services rendered or gifts given in the past. The virgin is not a commodity, as I have already shown by contrasting *sampradān* to *pon,* the latter being a *dābi,* a rightful demand which is made before accepting the virgin. The double gift made by the bride's father is the basis of the alliance system.

The gifts of virgin and dowry do not exhaust the range of exchanges in marriage. *Paona, dān,* and *upahār* are all culturally defined gifts associated with the various stages of the rituals. In much of the marriage literature, these gifts and prestations are said to be tied to hypergamy.[12] The lack of symmetry in gift giving is seen as being due to the higher status of those to whom one always gives brides but from whom one never receives women in return. This is not the case in Bengal, however, where there are exchange marriages and where certain exchanges in the course of the rituals are quite unrelated to hypergamy. The *paona*s are particularly relevant to understanding the rituals (especially the *strī ācār*s), women's role in the *śvaśur bāṛi,* and the relation between *jajmān* and *prajā* (the system of ritual and other services rendered by specialized castes to a household on a regular basis). *Paona*s and *dān*s are equally important in understanding *pāṛā* (neighborhood) organization, the bonds between the living and the dead (ancestors) and other deities, women and their children, and the maintenance as well as the definition of the links among relatives (*āttiya, kuṭum, śvaśur lok*—in-laws' people, *jñati*).

The pattern of gift giving in marriage defines and expresses an indigenous domain of kinship.[13] I am not concerned here with the definition of Bengali kinship except insofar as the understanding of kinship illuminates the full significance of *paona* and *dān,* the relations between the houses of in-laws, the hierarchy of women in the house, and the equivalence as well as status difference (in the rites themselves) between the givers and takers of gifts. I have already discussed relationships among persons, both in the Bengali construction of the person and in the classes of persons participating in marriage alliance. I have also noted the significance of marriage for the notion of the person, line, and house, as well as *jñati* and *kuṭum*. We now have to enter into further detail about the classes of relatives involved in ritual action.

A relationship as such is *samparka* or *sambandha*. The former refers to a link between persons, so *madhur samparka* is a sweet, loving relationship, whereas *lajjā samparka* is one of avoidance and shyness. These relations characterize the ties between MB-ZS and BW-HB respectively. *Sambandha,* however, refers to a relation specifically through marriage. A *sambandhī* is the most important *kuṭum*: the brother-in-law. In the marriage rites this class of people is even more important than *jñati.* Only those *jñati* with whom there are "sweet" relations are invited, whereas all *sambandhī* relatives (so referred to) have to be present. In addition, anyone with a close relationship to the house is expected to come to reaffirm ties. One shares something with all these people; they are *āttiya* of sorts. Thus it is not merely consanguinity and affinity but nearness and farness—kind of *samparka, sambandha, biye,* and *rakta*—that include or exclude persons in and from other classes within the larger discrimination of *āttiya*/non-*āttiya*.

Whereas *āttiya* are all of one's own people, *jñati* and *kuṭum* are, as I have said, more restricted classes within *āttiya. Rakta āttiya* and *jñati* are opposed to *kuṭum,* all of whom are "own" in opposition to those who are *āttiya* in relationship only. Two lines or houses that exchange daughters in marriage or are otherwise in an alliance relationship are *kuṭum* to each other. As such, all *kuṭum* are opposed to *jñati* (those with whom one shares *gotra*), *bhāiyat* (those related through male ties), *sātpuruṣ* (those related in the seven generations of men), and *sapiṇḍa* (those to whom funeral offerings are due). *Kuṭum,* however, become *jñati* through succeeding generations: *śālā,* WB becomes *māmā,* MB.

Kuṭum par excellence are one's *jāmāi* (DH) and *śālā* (WB). Again, because of the nature of blood and the meaning of marriage as a sacred union, a *jāmāi* is counted as an *āttiya* and not only as a *kuṭum;* he is the point where the alliance joins two lines. Hence, he is the foremost *kuṭum.* A *boumā* (SW) is *āttiya* to her in-laws, but a SWM-F is related by marriage. The further giving of daughters is therefore possible for both groups of *kuṭum* since no *gotra* and *jñati* ties act as barriers to further exchanges. The *jāmāi* who forges the link between two lines is a blood relative only to his father's group. Since he is an *āttiya* to both lines, blood is not the basis of the *āttiya* tie; rather, it is the construction of sameness (out of several possible ways of sharing) that is the essence of the *āttiya* category.

Kuṭum ties are extended through marriage relations, wife-takers as well as the takers of takers being *kuṭum*. But where *āttiya* is opposed to *kuṭum* it is in reference to the nearness of the relationship ego to which *kuṭum* is applied; thus *jāmāi* is the only *āttiya* who is not a blood or *jñati* relative. A bride acquires new *jñati* through marriage, which instantly changes her group of *jñati*. Her husband's *āttiya* and *jñati* become her own people, though these same people remain *kuṭum* to her father's house. Her *nanod*, HZ, is a sister to her, and H/B are brothers to her. But they are *bhāiyat* relatives, not *rakta* relations. The tie is a "brother" tie, but not a "blood-brother" tie. The crucial point here is the bride's change of *gotra*: women acquire these new relatives through *gotra* and not via transubstantiation. The bride retains her own father's blood; otherwise she would not be able to carry on her husband's line.

Paona, Dān, and *Upahār*

*Paona*s are not voluntary gifts. Rather, they are demanded by the receiver as obligatory payments for services that are about to be performed or that have been given repeatedly in the past. The pattern of giving exhibits the division of labor entailed by the caste system. *Paona*s are dues for *jāti* functions, especially those performed in the context of life cycle rituals. At marriage, *paona*s are given to the Dom (basketmaker and musician), the male and female Nāpit (barber), and the Brāhmaṇ ritualists (different classes of Brāhmaṇs act as priests, preceptors, and cooks). Each of the five *mugla*s (a group of *strī ācār*s that bestow blessings) are accompanied by *paona*s from the *jajmān* to the persons involved. These rites revolve around the cooking hearth, the barber's kit (used to beautify women), the drum used in ceremonies and in recreation, the rice-husking pedal, the grinding stone and pestle used for crushing spices, and the bowl of dried legumes used in the preparation of *dal* (which forms, together with rice, the staple diet of Bengalis). In the *nāndīmukh* offerings to one's ancestors and deities, the priest receives the *paona*s. The *snān* (bath) *paona* is due to the Nāpit after the bride and groom take their first bath (for purification, in the context of the marriage rite). The bride's father has to provide *paona*s to *kuṭum* to show the respect due to all *kuṭum*. Thus *paona*s are given to the groom's MB, the groom himself, and to the husbands of married daughters as the first and most deserving among the *kuṭum*.

The size of the gift varies from house to house. It may range from a mound of rice and a few coins to expensive *sāri*s and *dhoti*s (apparel worn by women and men) and elaborate meals. Token gifts may be given to the midwife (Dāimā) and the washerman (Dhobā), although the two do not have specific ritual duties at the marriage ceremony. The midwife may accompany the bride on her first journey to the in-laws' house, especially if the bride is still a child; for this she is given special *paona*s. The *nitkanyā*, a small girl dressed as a bride and in constant attendance on the bride, is given a *paona* by the groom's people.

The caste functions are performed by those associated with the house and line through links which may go back several generations. No outsiders may be called in, so the line's habitual barber, washerman, and priest must perform the necessary services. The gifts are dispensed by the *ginnīmā* (mistress of the house) before or after the rituals are performed. The caste *paona*s are all associated with purity and pollution: washing and bathing, shaving, and the paring of nails by the Nāpit are purificatory rites. Also related to purity is the notion of auspiciousness in applying lac to women's feet and in using various auspicious objects. The *mugla*s express desires for the happiness of the household and the gods' blessings on one's close relatives. These expectations of *maṅgal kāmonā* (auspicious blessings) are the work of the ritual. The ritual achieves its goal through the proper observance of the various actions, the use of required objects, and the participation of the prescribed persons. Since peace and harmony should reign in the performance of an auspicious rite such as marriage, the *paona*s must not only be given but should also be graciously accepted. A refusal is in itself inauspicious (*amaṅgal*). Although there should be no nagging, a *ginnīmā* will try to increase the *paona* should it be found meager.

Dān, which is also a gift, is bestowed upon rather than demanded by the receiver. There is no reciprocal obligation on the part of the receiver. *Dān* is given by a father to a married daughter and by a bride to her *śāsuṛī* on first entering the in-laws' house. *Dān* is expected but this does not dictate the giving or the choice of the goods. It is expected that a father will send the bride to her *śvaśur bāṛi* with a *dān* of kitchen utensils, but this is not a *dābi* on the groom's behalf. The gift of a pair of conch-shell bangles given by father to bride in the rite of *śaṅkha paṛāna* (wearing-the-shell) is also a *dān*. The three *sāri*s given during the central marriage rites are *dān*s symbolizing the bride's change of status. The *rakta sāri* is given by the bride's father and worn for auspiciousness during the rituals. The *lajjā* (avoidance and shyness) *sāri* is given by the bride's in-laws and worn during the crucial moment of *sindūr dān* (a high moment of the rituals when the groom puts vermilion into the parting of the bride's hair). Finally, the *bhāt kapar* ('rice clothes'—a *sāri*) is given by the groom to his wife, establishing the husband's and the line's relation to the wife.

One of the most significant *dān*s is the bride's gift to the father-in-law (*śvaśur*), the *kanyā kañjali*. This gift expresses most clearly the role the incoming wife of the line is to play in her new house as against her continuing relation to her father's house. A series of other *dān*s going from the groom's side to the bride and her side (*āltā sāri, śaṅkha sāri*) also reveals the changes in the bride's status and the meanings of the relations among persons.

*Upahār*s are presents. Relatives make small gifts on first seeing the bride's or groom's face and on first seeing them after the completion of the *mukh dekhā* (seeing the face) rituals. These are given at the *bāsar ghar*[14] in the bride's house and at the groom's house on the day of *bou bhāt* (the first rice served by the bride in the groom's house). Various presents are given at the different *āśīrbād*s (blessings performed at both bride's and groom's houses) to the bride and groom by senior relatives before and after the marriage rituals.

A separate class of presents is formed by the various *tattva*s, gifts exchanged between the houses of bride and groom in the context of certain rituals. An example is the *gāe halud tattva,* a present from the groom's house to the bride preceding the auspicious rite of smearing the bride with turmeric. This gift the bride takes with her when she goes to her in-laws' house, whereas the *tattva*s given to the groom by the bride's house are meant to be kept.

The Five Auspicious Rites

*Mugla*s, "auspicious rites," deal with women and the *saṇgsār,* and they are performed by married women. Women say that the *saṇgsār* is destroyed when the rice vessels of a house are empty. But just as the pots should be full of wealth, so should the *saṇgsār pata* (the living members of the household) be numerous, given that children represent the wealth of the *baṇgśa.* Empty vessels parallel barren women, for both mark the ruin of a line. Thus, married women worship both Lakṣmī and Ṣaṣṭhī. Women cannot worship these deities in their father's house; they begin the worship after marriage, for it is the husband's line and wealth they must increase and maintain. All the myths married women recite and the rites they perform during the ritual cycle revolve around these central symbols of *saṇgsār*.

The *ginnīmā* performs most of the rites, but she can ask the Brāhmaṇ to perform them on her behalf. These rituals do not, however, require the services of the Brāhmaṇ, nor can they be found in the Śāstras (sacred texts). They are *procalita ācār*s, locally practiced customs, without the incantations (*mantra*s) and other paraphernalia of Brahmanic ritual. They relate to the world of women but their symbolism belongs to society as a whole, even if on a level different from that of the major Brahmanic ritual cycles.

The *ḍheki* (husking-paddle) *mugla* (blessing) is performed a few days before the marriage. The *ḍheki* is blessed because it is to be used to grind all the spices and pulses necessary for cooking meals for the entire period during which the marriage rituals take place and some spices for use in the other rituals. This grinding involves enormous labor. Already ground spices and pulses are available from the market, yet for the marriage rites the *ḍheki* has to be used. The ordinary grinding stone and pestle (*śil noṛā*) are considered inadequate for the task. Houses without a *ḍheki* borrow a neighbor's. It is especially auspicious to use the *ḍheki* of a higher caste household. Once the work is begun it must be finished, since it is inauspicious for the *ḍheki* to break down or for the work to be left incomplete. Because work is undertaken on behalf of one's *kuṭum* and *jñati*, all aspects of the preparation must show respect for one's relatives, some of whom are asked to help and have to be fed.

The mistress of the house (*ginnī*) performs the whole rite without a Brāhmaṇ priest. She begins the blessing by doing obeisance to the *ḍheki*. Having changed her overnight *sāri* and having taken a purifying bath, she cleans and purifies the *ḍheki* with water and the adjacent ground with cow dung and water to make them pure for the ritual. She then takes a brass plate, turmeric, vermilion paste, oil, flowers, and a few coins and makes a series of offerings to the *ḍheki*. Kneeling and squatting on her heels, she applies five or seven marks (*phota*) of turmeric, vermilion, and oil to the *ḍheki*. Placing some flowers on the grinder, she sprinkles holy water (*sānti jal*, 'peace-water,' reviously blessed) and then bends forward, touching her forehead to the ground in an expression of profound respect also used in encountering the gods (in both cases, the act is called *praṇām*). With the rite performed, the *ginnī* gives the *paona* to the person who is to grind the spices—in this case the Nāpit (barber) woman, whose only role in the blessing itself is the acceptance of the *paona*. The objects given (a pound of rice, oil for the hair, and some money) are regarded as mere tokens (*sida*).

Camlatalā, showing the *alpanā* design, the *śil/norā* and the two *piṛi*.

The *ḍhol mugla* is similar to the *ḍheki mugla* except that it is performed in front of the *ḍhol* (a large two-ended drum) brought by a Ḍom woman or man to be played for the wedding. Doms, a caste of basket weavers, have to supply different kinds of wicker baskets needed for the rituals. One is the *lotā* for the thread which is wound around the four auspicious clay pots (*ak hāṛis*) on the *camlatalā*, the altar platform around which all the sacred acts of the the marriage take place. Then there is a container for the *tapar*, the crownlike headdress worn by the groom. Other baskets (*ghuris*) serve as containers for other items. All these wicker products are available in the bazaar, and if the Dom doesn't weave them himself he can purchase and bring them to the house, where the *ginnī* will reimburse him. When the baskets have been brought and the *ḍhol* has been blessed, the Dom also receives *paona*.

The Dom plays the drum during the performance of the *mugla*, and he stays in the house for the duration of the marriage, if the household can afford it, to play every time a new ritual begins. The drum announces that a *śubha kāj* (auspicious work) is about to be performed. Drumming accompanies the small processions involved in the various women's rites such as going to the *ghāt* to bathe the bride, fetching the *nisi* (fresh water) for the rites after the marriage itself is over, and bringing the *ak hāṛis* from the Kumār's (potter's) house. Drumming precedes every *strī ācār* as well as the high moments of the marriage such as *māla badal* (the exchange of garlands) and *sindūr dān* (the application of vermilion to the bride's forehead). The sound of the drum is accompanied by the buglelike call of the sacred conch shell (blown by women), a sound equally auspicious and produced for the same reason. Being made of leather, the drum itself is impure, yet it produces auspiciousness, and the *ginnī* touches it with reverence this day. In wealthy households the drum is complemented by bands of musicians or local jazz bands such as the Izzat Band or the Calcutta Highlights Band.

The *dābi mugla* is the blessing of the Nāpit's (barber's) shaving kit, which precedes the barber's participation in the rituals. Women participating in all the rituals have to be purified by having their nails cut and *āltā* (red lac) applied to their feet by the Nāpit woman.[15] The Nāpit is also sent to bring the women needed for the rites to the bride's house so that all may go through *kāmāno* (purifying) together. The women thus invited are very close to the house, either *nikaṭ āttiya* or *āttiya*-like persons whether or not they are of the same caste. Women asked to participate in the *strī ācār*s have a sweet (*madhu*) relation to the *ginnīmā,* and being set apart from the ordinary invitees (who are sent cards asking them to attend the major rites of the marriage), they have an important kinship role to play. The presence of women in *madhur samparka* to the bride's house is auspicious, and the loving, sweet relations are expected to turn into blessings for the young couple. The women present are regarded as mothers or mother's sisters to the bride.

The *ginnī* performs this *mugla* in the usual manner by marking the Nāpit's kit with vermilion. When the rite is finished she takes the kit to the *Kubi ghar,* a small altar built for the Lord Kuber, the treasurer of the gods and the lord of wealth. The kit is placed in front of the *Kubi pāṭā,* a representation of Kuber. Doing *praṇām,* the lady of the house prays that the *kāmāno* goes well, the barber does her job properly, all be purified so that the gods may be pleased, bride and groom be pure for marriage, and all results be auspicious. The Nāpit may now have her kit back, receive her *paona,* and start her work.

The barbers have the most important caste function in the *mugla*s and the barber's *paona* is always more than that of the Dom or

Kāmāno: a woman barber helps purify the women.

midwife. *Kāmāno* is a significant component of all life cycle rites, especially those most polluting, the actions surrounding death. In ritual contexts the Nāpit is a purifier; her touch will not pollute higher castes. The women can take the purifying bath before the Nāpit clips their nails. Doing her purifying work, the Nāpit woman faces south and uses a small blade, cotton dipped in *āltā*, and a stone to scrape the soles of the feet. The first to be attended to is a Brāhmaṇ woman. If it is a non-Brāhmaṇ household, then a Brāhmaṇ woman is invited and she will be asked to start off all the *strī ācār*s, receiving a *paona* in each rite. This custom is both a reflection of Brāhmaṇ status in the caste system and a Sanscritizing tendency which brings more of the women's rites into the high Brahmanic context. After this, all the women of the house and the married women of the *strī ācār*s are served by the barber.

The process of *kāmāno* is simple. The Nāpit always starts with the nails of the hand, left to right, going on to the feet in the same manner. Even if the nails need no cutting she touches them with her knife for purification. *Āltā* is applied to the feet, but it is also touched to the bangles married women wear, to the tips of the fingers, and to the conch shell, all of which are auspicious things for women. Having been purified, the women do *praṇām* to the barber. The same process is repeated—though more elaborately—with the bride the day before the marriage. At the same time, the groom is attended in his house by the Nāpit of his line. Items such as the leaf (*pātā*) on which bride and groom stand while being served, the cotton used for applying *āltā,* and other objects used in the rites are kept for one year after the marriage (when the couple is considered to be beyond the reach of any inauspicious or evil influence)[16] and then immersed in an open body of water. The Nāpit of the groom's house accompanies the *bār jātri* (groom's party) to the bride's house and assists the priests (*kulapurohit*s) of both the bride's and the groom's houses during the rituals.

The Nāpit receives the *sāri* and *dhoti* worn by bride and groom at the time of their first bath after the marriage. Purifying bride and groom needs no *mugla,* yet the barber gets all the *paona*s. The Nāpit sets up the *camlatalā* for the rituals. If the barber himself is polluted (by a birth or a death), he can send a replacement.[17] Among the lowest castes the work of the barber is performed by the sister's husband or the equivalent.

The *onan mugla* is the blessing performed for the cooking hearth (*onan*) before the Brāhmaṇ begins to cook for the marriage feast; the blessing is similar to the *ḍheki mugla.* The *onan* is specially built in the courtyard, larger than the ordinary oven, but like it, made of clay with a fire pit underground and a round wall to support huge cauldrons. Size is not the only reason for a new hearth; food cooked in non-Brāhmaṇ houses may not be acceptable to other castes—hence the necessity of a new oven and a Brāhmaṇ cook. The Brāhmaṇ also serves the food. Brāhmaṇs will cook and serve for the high and mid-ranking castes. Low castes use the services of their own caste priests. The preparations for all meals and rites are made, as much as possible, in the household.

Once the *mugla* has been performed by the *ginnī* for the *onan,* the Brāhmaṇs can commence cooking. The usual marriage food is *pulau* rice or fried wheat cakes with meat, fish, and vegetable curries, followed by sweets and *pān* (betel leaf). The ingredients are prepared by the women of the house, but since only the Brāhmaṇ can touch the utensils, he has to put all the ingredients into the pot himself. The Brāhmaṇs also serve the meals of the day to the household, the women gathered for the *strī ācār*s, and the relatives arriving before the marriage. But the evening feast itself is the most important. It has to be pure as well as tasty, for the meal itself expresses the respect in which the house holds its *kuṭum lok* (*kuṭum* people). This being a happy (*śubha,* "auspicious") day, the *kuṭum* and *jñati* have to be satisfied. If there is a mishap in the cooking, an impurity or lack of quality and quantity which may cause guests to leave in anger, then the resulting *amaṅgal* (inauspiciousness) will affect the house as well as the bride and groom.[18]

The last *mugla,* the *kalāi mugla,* is performed just before the Brāhmaṇ does the *nāndīmukh,* the rite honoring the ancestors. The *kalāi mugla* is different from the others in that it requires the participation of five or seven (or rarely, nine), married women, the number coinciding with the number of days birth pollution is observed in the house. The husbands of these five or seven women should be living and not previously married to other women. The women have witnessed all the *mugla*s but are active only in this last *mugla* before the marriage is completed. *Kalāi mugla* is meant to accomplish two things: first, to introduce bride and groom to the *saṇgsār* (everyday life); second, to reaffirm ties among persons. The *mugla* uses many objects women use in everyday life, but in a different way, to express the ideals of womanhood and the central role of women in the *saṇgsār.*

The *kalāi mugla* is a joyous event during which drums are beaten and conch shells are blown to announce the occasion. The preparations for it take place over a period of days. They begin when bride and groom sit in front of the *camlatalā* in their separate households, and a Brāhmaṇ woman or the *ginnī* pours mustard oil into brass spoonlike objects (*kosakusi,* vessels used in temple rituals). She then places *kalā* (a type of legume), rice, and five or seven whole pieces of turmeric on a brass plate and betel leaves and nuts on the ground. She then puts the plate in front of the couple and holds a *pān* with a nut to their foreheads, the point of the leaf in a skyward direction. First the *ginnī,* then the women one by one, pour oil onto the betel leaf and the heads of the young couple; and as the oil drips down into the plate of *kalāi,* the bride and groom mix oil and pulses together. Each woman repeats the act five times. The rite over, the couple shred the *pān* and do *praṇām* to the *ginnī.* The *ginnī* then covers their heads with the end (*ācal*) of her *sāri* and takes them to the *Kubi ghar,* where they do *praṇām* to the Lord Kuber before they are uncovered again.[19] The women, in ceremonial procession, bring the four auspicious pots (*ak hāṛis*) and pour the mixture of oil and legumes into them. The pots are then returned to the four corners of the *camlatalā.* These pots are usually brought from the potter's house but they can come from a Bene (trader caste) and they may be kept

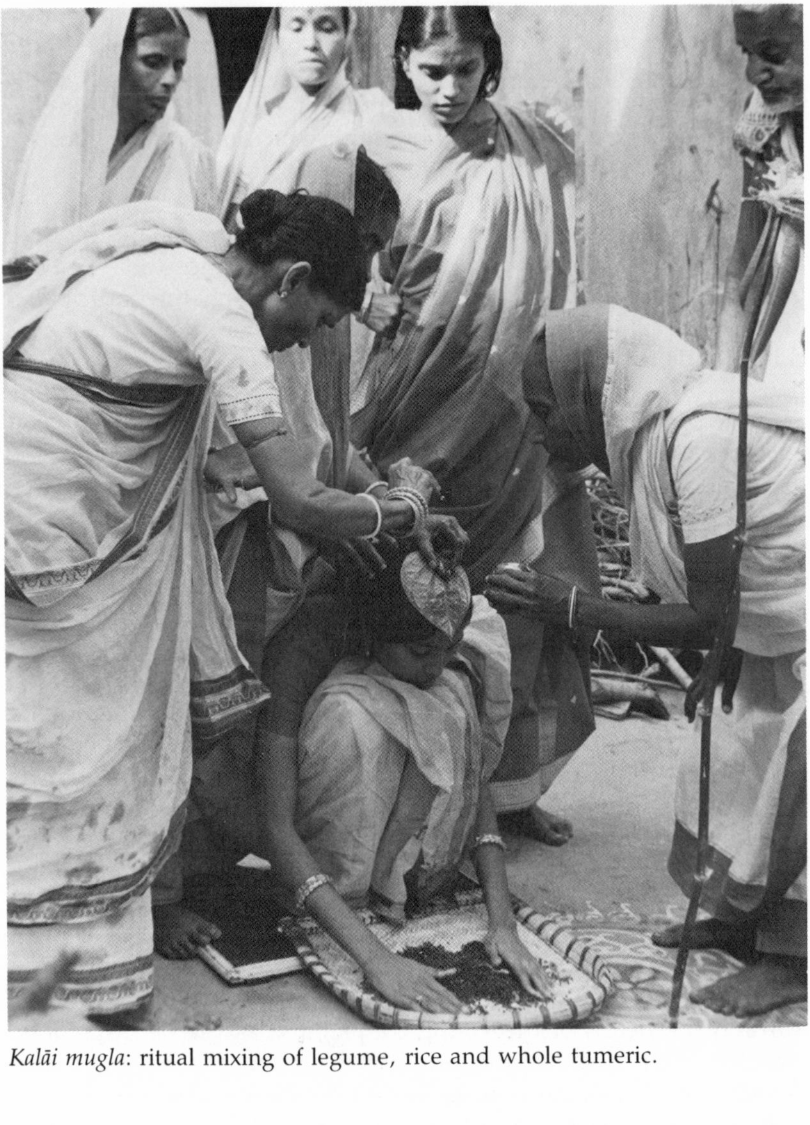

Kalāi mugla: ritual mixing of legume, rice and whole tumeric.

in the house of a Brāhmaṇ for a few days before the marriage. *Paonas* are given to all those involved in these transactions. Married women put vermilion on each other's shell bangles on each of these encounters.

The four pots with the *kalāi* inside are covered and kept in the *camlatalā* for eight days, until the *aṣṭamaṅgala* (the *maṅgala*, or *mugla*,

Kalāi mugla: oil is poured on the *pān* leaf and it drips into the plate with the pulses.

of the eighth day), when the bride and groom return to the bride's father's house for this ritual. That day, the bride and groom come to the *camlatalā,* the groom opening and the bride closing the pots, asking, in turn, "Whose face am I seeing?" and uttering each other's names in silence.[20] This is repeated five or seven times. The pots are full of *kalāi,* rice, oil, and turmeric. Rice (*dhān,* "unhusked rice") represents wealth (*dhan*) as property and as the issue of a line (*santān,* "offspring"). (Wet *kalāi* is offered to Ṣaṣṭhī, the Goddess of Children, in other contexts.) The couple look into the full pots so that all the rice vessels of their house will remain full. They see each others' wealth in the pots, and each others' face. Indeed, each *is* wealth to the other. A married woman is "rich" to have fulfilled the ideal of girlhood, in starting a new *baṇgśa.* The groom is bringing wealth into his house in a double sense: first, by bringing a working girl to his parents; second, by bringing someone who will bear a son—the main reason (*adisthān*) and right (*adhikār*) of marriage. Then there is also the material wealth of the dowry.

On the ninth day after the *biye,* just before the *kalāi mugla,* a small child is made to sit on the lap of both bride and groom. Bride and child stand for Ṣaṣṭhī and her children, just as the ordinary pestle and grinding stone (*śil noṛā*) represent Ṣaṣṭhī and her 60 children. The assembled women, *kuṭum, jñati,* and neighbors are all present to ask Ṣaṣṭhī to bestow the boon of a new male line on the couple. The married women, all of whom have living husbands so that the bride may herself participate in many such rituals during a long married life, then boil the *kalāi* without salt, as a pure offering, and eat it themselves. The couple cannot eat of this since it symbolizes their *phol,* the many kinds of wealth asked from the Lord Kuber and the Goddess Ṣaṣṭhī.

The *kalāi mugla* is a celebration of the married woman. Virgins are excluded, but the rites resemble those performed for girls when they first menstruate. In the *punar* (menstrual) *biye* (marriage) rites the young girl is also seated with a child on her lap and is offered fruit, which she distributes to other children, since she cannot eat of her own fruit (*phol*). The place of the child may be taken by the grinding stone without the pestle. There are also parallels with other life cycle rites, especially with those at the time of birth, when on the eighth day the mother is offered *kalāi,* which she cannot eat.

The Gifts of the Bride to Her Father and Father-in-law

I have established so far that marriage is a time for gift exchanges among persons sharing caste or kin relations indigenously defined and that marriage itself is the most sacred gift a man can make. The rituals not only express a *kuṭum* status or a definition of *saṇgsār* but construct these meanings in the very acts of the performance. In the giving of gift's, the giver, receiver, and object are all significant; each is suspended in a context of ritual actions as well as relationships extending to other domains of life. It is through a pursuit of these interconnections that the full meaning of rites such as *kalāi mugla* and of participants such as "married women" (*strīs*) really emerges. The gifts given and received in the ritual context also define and in turn are defined by the kinship relation between the persons involved. Often marriage is the only time when such encounters take place, and it is here that the relationship is rendered meaningful.

The rite of *kanyā kañjali* is as significant as the *kalāi mugla*. The two rituals express a concern for *baṇgśa*; they involve the same deities; and they are related to the worship of the ancestors in the main marriage rite. They also bring together the father and his house, and the father-in-law and his house in the symbolism and performance of the rituals.

Kanyā means "daughter, bride"; *kañjali* means a "respectful offering," one that is given to elders (*gurujan*) and gods (*añjali* is a flower offering to deities). The term covers the gifts of the bride to her father on the day of her departure after the marriage and to her father-in-law on the day of her welcoming rituals in her new home. The offering to the father is in return for all the past care, love, food, and clothing he gave to his daughter. A daughter owes (*sodh karā*) something to her father, but after marriage she belongs to a different house. Before leaving, the daughter makes a gift that symbolizes the separation from her previous life. The offering is a pound of rice, betel nut, coins, and a small pile of earth dug out of a mousehole (*iñdur māṭi*, "the earth of a mouse"). The bride takes a handful of the rice and handing it to her father says, "Here, take this, for all that I consumed in your house." She repeats this three times and each time the father accepts the rice and then puts it back on the plate. Finally the bride does *praṇām* to the father, touching his feet in obeisance.

She carries the same plate to her father-in-law's house and makes a similar gift of it to the groom's father. She is now in her *śvaśur*'s house, where the future responsibility for feeding and clothing her is that of her father-in-law. In turn, she has to attend to her new *saṇgsār*, providing its members with services, care, and love (both devotion and respect, *bhakti* and *sammān*). Thus, she acquires a new code of conduct when she changes her residence after marriage. The same gift given to the two types of father expresses the change of *saṇgsār*, past and future, and the roles played and to be played in them. Now she gives the rice she brings from her father's house in return for her future dependency on her new people (*śvaśur lok*).

The departure and farewell (*bidai*) of the bride is a tearful affair. The bride's parents experience sorrow even though the journey (*jātrā*) is an auspicious (*śubha*) one leading to a new life. The place of a woman is now in her *śvaśur bāṛi* (in-laws' house), no longer in her *bāper bāṛi* (father's house). Mothers cry on the departure of their daughters, for the link through one's *nāṛi* (navel, umbilical cord) cannot be forged with new daughters, the incoming wives of one's sons. This final journey of the bride from her father's responsibility (*dahitta*) is a "journey" in many ways. It is a change of residence, of responsibility, of life cycle stages (*jiban jātrā*, "journey through life"). The gift itself is symbolic of a journey and of the journeys a married woman continues to make between the houses of her father and in-laws. For although she is now of another house, the married woman remains linked to her father's house even if in ways entirely different from those of her maiden days. Her father's house, where her brothers stay, will become *māmā bāṛi* (MB's house) to her children.

So when she comes to her father-in-law for the first time, she bears the gifts that symbolize the wealth she consumed in her *bāper bāṛi*. The earth from the mousehole expresses the married woman's life. She moves from house to house, shifting wealth from one to the other, just as the mouse shifts earth. Earth stands for the wealth she is bringing to her father-in-law, for she moves her father's wealth to the house of her in-laws. Gifts are made to her on every occasion she visits her *bāper bāṛi*. Her brothers will continue the pattern of giving in relation to her children. The wealth goes to the bride-takers, completing the alliance established by the gift of the virgin.

When the couple arrives in the groom's father's house, they are greeted as deities. In the welcoming rituals the bride is Lakṣmī, the Goddess of Wealth. The plate of rice and earth in her hands, the bride represents (to her *śvaśur śāsuṛī*) the Goddess Lakṣmī, holding the attributes of wealth. In a second, sacred sense of the gift, she comes as a relative to a new set of kinsmen, a relative capable of increasing the wealth (sons, in this case) of the line. In return the bride receives a husband. Her gift to her in-laws is that of a *boumā* (SW), reciprocating the gift of a husband. The *kanyā kañjali* in this context is a *dān* as well as a *paona* to the in-laws for being accepted into the new house. The wealth she brings with her is shared by the whole house and may be contributed to the marriages of the virgin daughters in the house. The latter in turn will take that wealth to their in-laws' houses. Women are indeed movers of wealth; what they bring they also take away. But the other wealth, the children of the line, remains, and this is of the greatest significance to the house.

The *Bastra* Gift

The gift of *bastra* (clothes, *sāri*s) to the bride and the ritual context in which they are given express and establish a new relationship to a new set of relatives in addition to accomplishing significant changes in the bride's status as the marriage ceremonies unfold. First, the *rakta bastra* (blood *sāri*) is given to the bride by her father. Red is an auspicious color associated with married women, who wear vermilion in the parting of their hair, *āltā* on their feet, and red-bordered *sāri*s in everyday life (widows have to wear white all the time). The *rakta bastra* is the father's last gift, his last *adhikār* (right, responsibility) to an unmarried daughter. The daughter thus attired represents the status, prestige, and purity of the father's line in front of the assembled *jñati* and *kuṭum*. This is the moment when the father finally relinquishes his responsibility for his daughter and transfers her to another *saṇgsār* and *paribār*.

The *lajjā bastra* (the *sāri* of withdrawal and shyness) is given to the bride by the groom's side just before the *sindūr dān* (gift of vermilion), the rite that confirms the virgin's married status. In this rite the groom applies *sindūr* three times to the parting of the bride's hair, a sign of marriage she will continue to apply herself as long as her husband is alive. The *lajjā bastra* is used to cover the bride during the *sindūr dān*. This expresses the bride's shyness at being married and facing all the relatives. As such, she will always have to show respect to the in-laws and be humble in the presence of *śvaśur śāsuṛī*. The *lajjā bastra* also represents the *ācal*, the end part of the *sāri* used to cover the head as a sign of withdrawal and humility. The practice of *ghomṭā* is a feature of everyday life and as such signifies a kind of avoidance relationship between the bride and certain persons in the *śvaśur bāṛi*. A young wife puts on the *ghomṭā* when she is in the presence of her *gurujan*, her HF-HM, HeB, and her HMB. The *lajjā bastra* over her head, the bride becomes of the groom's line; her husband is now responsible for her purity and respect.

The *bhāt kapar* (rice clothes) is given to the bride on the day of *bou bhāt* (wife-rice), when she serves cooked rice to her *śvaśur lok* (in-laws) for the first time. This *sāri* is a gift from husband to wife. By wearing it, the bride accepts the duties and responsibilities of her new status in her new *saṇgsār paribār*. Her new responsibilities include the full care of the household and its people as well as its animals (cows and goats). But most important of all, she cooks rice—pure and nourishing food. If it is an *ekanna paribār* (joint family, literally, 'one-rice house'), she shares the responsibility for cooking with the other wives of the line. The husband, in turn, assumes the care, protection, feeding, and clothing of the wife. He is now the provider of his own small *paribār* and house. Thus the husband's roles and statuses also change as a result of marriage. The *bou bhāt* signifies the acceptance of the bride as a full participant in *bhāiyat* and *jñati* groups. It also expresses her acceptance by the local *jāti* group and by the *kuṭum* of her new house. Now and only now that marriage is complete, can it be consummated.

Several gifts of clothes given by the bride to her new relatives remain to be discussed. These are the *praṇāmi,* or *namaskāri, kapar* (clothes). *Praṇām* is deep obeisance, touching the feet of another in respect. *Namaskār* is a simpler way of showing respect: bringing the palms together in front of one's heart or forehead. Entering the in-laws' house for the first time, the bride does *praṇām* to the elders and gives them gifts of clothing (*sāri*s for women, *dhoti*s for men). The number of *kapar* given depends on the economic condition of the bride's father's house. Gifts may be given only to the closest relatives: HF-HM and HFBW. They may also be given to all the married daughters of the house and their husbands. The list of relatives in the in-laws' house is given to the bride's house long before the marriage. The quality of the gifts varies; some are silk, others are cotton. The gift establishes the relationship of the bride to the receiver for a lifetime. The *praṇām* expresses a respect relation even though no reciprocal gifts are made by the groom's side.

The bride stands in a hierarchical relation to the elders of her *śvaśur bāṛi.* She does *praṇām* to the HeB (*bhāśur*) on some occasions and avoids him on others. Terminologically, the relation to the HeBW, however, is a fully reciprocal one, both being *jā* to each other. The HyB (*deor*) and his wife (*nanod*) are also in a sweet, joking relation to the bride. All younger categories of persons treat the bride as an elder sister. These relatives (HyB, HyBW, HyZ) do not get *praṇāmi kapar.* Instead, they receive small gifts (e.g., cosmetics), items that do not express the hierarchical respect due to *gurujan* alone.

As brother's wife (*boudī*) the bride occupies a mediating position in her new house. The younger set of the house approach her in all their joys and troubles. Her relation to the elders, however, is one of submission. The *praṇāmi* gifts express the difference: the clothes themselves stand for respect and are given with *phota*s (marks) of turmeric and vermilion known as *kar* (invocation or invitation). The bride invokes or initiates a new set of relationships on her first day in the in-laws' house. This is parallel to the invocation of deities in temple rituals when the gods are asked to participate in the *pūjā* (offering) with the people of the locality. The bride "invokes" the elders in their new roles to her for the auspicious participation of all persons in the *saṇgsār*. She introduces herself as a new person in relation to her new roles, and they in turn accept her as an *āttiya*. She now becomes a *jñati* and *āttiya* of the *baṇgśa* in the fullest sense of the terms. This is the only time a bride offers gifts to her *śvaśur baṛī* people. The acceptance of the *praṇāmi* gift is the acceptance of the person. From now on they are her "own people." Further gifts have to come from *kuṭum*, from her father to her new *jñati*.

The bride's gifts represent an aspect of the continuing alliance between her father's and her father-in-law's house and lines. The gifts are alliance offerings, not presents to individuals, and they signal the *ādān pradān* arrangement. The nature of the gifts made expresses the interest and commitment the lines involved have to the possibility of future alliances, for either the flow of gifts may be reversed or more daughters may be given should the marriage experience prove satisfactory to all participants.

The Gifts to the Son-in-law

*Tattva*s are high-quality goods (e.g., umbrellas, golden rings, bags, shoes, shawls, and pants). Usually they are gifts from the bride's house to the groom. The only *tattva* given by the groom's house to the bride is the *gāe halud tattva* ('the gifts-of-the-smearing-of-turmeric-on-the-body'). These are items the bride needs for the *gāe halud* ritual, items of food for the day of the ritual, and other prestations for the bride. Since the *gāe halud tattva* is meant for the bride and not her household, utensils and other household items are never sent. Expensive food items such as fish form an important part of the *tattvas*.[21]

*Jāmāi tattva*s come in three divisions—*biye tattva* (at marriage) and summer and winter *tattva*s (things used in the appropriate season)—and may be given either all together or one at a time throughout the year following the marriage. They establish a son-in-law in the category of *āttiya* to the father and mother of the bride. The acceptance of the ongoing gift-giving relationship also confirms his *āttiya* status and maintains the alliance relationship to the rest of the house and line. The relation to the *jāmāi* is a special and respectful one. *Jāmāi*, an otherwise *kuṭum* category, is made into *āttiya* both through the marriage ritual (and the specific tie of *swāmī strī*) and through the continued giving of gifts. Throughout his life the *jāmāi* is given gifts, honor, and respect. He is invited to all life cycle rituals and major annual calendrical feasts of the house. On each occasion he is served the best food and receives the best gifts. The *jāmāi* has to be pampered, for if relations go sour, the daughter of the house is forever lost to her parents. A satisfied *jāmāi* ensures a good position for the daughter of the house in the *śvaśur bāṛi*. This way, the married daughter may continue to visit her father's house.[22]

The *jāmāi* is asked to his father-in-law's house on many occasions. The annual Durgā *pūjā* (the most important Bengali festival, the celebrations of the Mother Goddess), Jāmāi Ṣaṣṭhī (the festival of the Goddess Ṣaṣṭhī, devoted to honoring the *jāmāi*), and other festivals find the *jāmāi* in the bride's house, plied with excellent food and good presents. The *jāmāi* does indeed become an *āttiya*; he participates in decisions concerning the house, most important of which are negotiating marriages for daughters of the house and finding brides for the sons.

Jāmāi bhanga, the rite "breaking" the son-in-law relationship, is performed on the eighth day of marriage. With this ritual the *jāmāi* acquires his *āttiya* status; he is no longer a *kuṭum*. This is the day when a *jāmāi* receives his *tattva*s and when other auspicious rituals are performed (especially the *aṣṭamaṅgala*). After the *jāmāi bhanga*, relations between *jāmāi* and the people of the bride's house become more relaxed and sweet (*madhu*). In this way the *jāmāi* achieves a status in his father-in-law's house similar (though hierarchically reverse) to that of the bride in her in-laws' house. There is, however, a difference: the *jāmāi* expects and receives special treatment even though he is not expected to take advantage of it.[23] To do so would mean losing respect (*sammān*) in the alliance relationship (*ādān pradān*). But the direction of the gift giving is clear: the flow of goods and respect is weighted in favor of the *śvaśur bāṛi*. There is a Bengali saying that one can never truly make a goldsmith, a sweetmaker, or a *jāmāi* one's own people. The goldsmith will cheat on the quality of the gold; the sweetmaker will save on the sugar; and the *jāmāi* will expect the best treatment and still complain about the difference between promise and performance.

CHAPTER 3

Betel Nuts, Cowries, and Turmeric: Married Women's Rituals in Marriage and Life

Other studies have treated marriage as a subset of more general rituals while treating women's rituals as a reflection of local caste and family organization. The procedure has been to look from caste to ritual, seeking a reflection of the former in the latter, and then to seek a residual domain—that of kinship—which is left over. My study reverses this customary direction. I proceed from the consideration of women's rituals to categories of action, to exegeses of rituals, to exchange among persons and groups, and ultimately to the domains in which all of these symbols, actions, and persons are enhanced with meaning. Thus there is no need to separate caste, kinship, and ritual; in my analysis all come together through cultural categories of women and marriage. The world of women is not just a sub-subset of local activity buried in each kinship group, beyond the pale of the Great Tradition and the really important problems of caste; it is perfectly feasible to arrive at the primary concerns of caste society—purity, hierarchy and equivalence, and the way people are related in hierarchy and equivalence—through a separate study of women and their ritual activities. It is possible, for example, to approach caste hierarchy through the domain of women's actions because some of the most central principles of Hindu society are manifested in marriage, the birth of a child, and the culturally determined transmission of elements making up the person.

In Chapters 1 and 2 I have demonstrated the complex interrelationships among caste, kinship, and ritual through analysis of the *paona, dān,* and *pon* exchanges and the *mugla* performances, all of which take place in the context of the marriage ceremonies. Caste and kinship principles were elucidated through women's rituals, the exchanges in them, and the cultural construction of those involved. Thus I have shown that marriage, birth, and the cultural meaning of blood are closely linked in the Bengali notion of the person and that, in turn, the classes of relatives reflect the composition of the person and the links by marriage and blood. Marriage expresses some of the categories of relatives and fashions or determines others, bringing all these categories into new relations with each other. In addition, I have shown how the terms for *female, married woman,* and *virgin* are not only defined by the symbolism of marriage but also acted out and created in the performance of women's rituals. What remains for me to explain is the world of women and women's rituals seen at the most local level, in the most private domain.

Married Women's Rites

Strī ācārs—married women's rites—exemplify the separateness as well as the complementarity of the women's world in relation to the whole Bengali society, just as this complementarity is also reflected in the rituals linking bride and groom to their respective in-laws' houses. A number of concerns find expression in the symbolism of marriage: the full meaning of the person; alliance for the construction of the person; the maintenance of future alliances; the generation of ties among relatives; and the key to an understanding of what the categories for "person" and "relative" mean, for example, the separateness and in-between position of women (as daughters and wives of line) as elaborated in the *iñdur māṭi* ritual of farewell and welcome, when a woman takes from her father to give to her father-in-law. A woman takes her *māṭr śakti* (female divine power) and her father's line and offers them to her father-in-law. The rites for welcoming the bride deify the married woman as a wife and potential mother. But a woman unmarried for too long, a barren woman, and a widow may be a curse to a house and line. These fears and concerns are expressed in the ritual play of women at the various stages of the marriage ceremony.

The position of women in Bengali society is not the subject symbolized in the rituals. It is, rather, the domain of women's action and concerns that these rituals symbolize, define, interpret, separate, and mark in relation to other domains. Rituals symbolize the principles of caste, purity, birth, and conception which enter into the construction of the person as well as caste and action in everyday life. Women are in this sense a world in themselves, one that is expressed, enacted, and constituted in the performance of women's rites and in the recitation of myths, legends, and stories (*brata kathā*) relating to the rituals.

The rites themselves *are* a reality, not just an idiom for the expression of reality (whether social structure, subordination, or local-level action). Time, energy, and money are spent on their performance, and they are intimately related to other rituals concerned with birth, death, the major annual festival cycles, and Hindu ideology as a whole. But most of all, women's rites and marriage embody the central symbols at the root of hierarchical action—purity/pollution, male/female—as well as the categories of *jāti, rakta, baṇgśa,* and classes of relatives and persons. The symbols and categories are themselves in a hierarchical relation to each other. The notion of femaleness in relation to maleness generates the notions of the person and of the relative.

The constituting principles of women's domain—purity, *śakti* (the power of femaleness), and *mātṛ śakti*—complement other principles of caste hierarchy such as *puruṣa.* Thus women are complementary, at the level of structure, to men, house, and line just as they are complementary to men in the conception and birth of a child and its introduction to the world at large. Conception and the cultural construction of the person form a set of meanings in which woman as mother and wife complements man as husband and male in symbolism as well as in action. The society (*samāj*) of women complements the whole of Bengali society at every turn. Brahmanic marriage rites are complemented by the *strī ācār*s, the rites being similar and the interpretations parallel even though the participation is quite different, for women are the ritualists in their own performances.

The term *strī* in *strī ācār* signifies "married woman." *Strī* as a cultural construct means "one's wife" (for a male) and signifies that one's husband (for a female) is still alive. *Strī* also means "female" in opposition to "male" (*strī lok,* women in general). *Nāṛi jāti* is another way of opposing male to female (*nāṛi* meaning "navel," "umbilical cord"; *jāti* meaning "kind" or "sort"). In the context of the rituals, married women are *eyo* or *eyo strī,* opposing their married state to that of widows, virgins, and men, who are all excluded from the performance of *strī ācār*s. The specific meanings of *strī* and *eyo* emerge in opposition to *bidhobā* (widow) and *kumāri* (virgin): the latter two are excluded from conception and birth, whereas the married woman is the potential mother of a son. Thus, once again the fullest meaning of "womanhood" is synonymous with "motherhood."

*Strī ācār*s are components of all life cycle rituals. In themselves they provide a peculiarly and specifically women's point of view. Not all *strī ācār*s are the same; those at marriage differ from those at birth, just as do the Brahmanic rites. At marriage, the emphasis is on the union and joining of male to female, line to line, house to house, bride to groom, mother to child. Birth rituals are concerned with the safety of mother and child and with the fear of death as a cutter of lines. The intent and purpose of women's rites changes from case to case, with the performance itself varying from caste to caste and house to house. Differences can be found between localities, lines, and segments of *jāti*. The overall significance of these rites for women need not blind us to the more conventional view of rituals as a marker for social structure. Viewing the rites in wider contexts makes it possible to link the women's domain to other domains, not just in terms of social morphology but in terms of meaning and category (as femaleness is linked to caste purity and hierarchy).

Although a Brāhmaṇ priest need not be present during *strī ācār*s, he can assist at some of the rites, Sanscritizing and Brahmanizing women's rituals, and this may be very important to lower caste women. It is, for instance, considered a sacred (*pabittra*) and auspicious act to ask a Brāhmaṇ to initiate the marriage *strī ācār*s by simply touching the bride and groom (beyond which he plays no further role in these rites), thereby setting the stage of the *eyo strī* to follow. Orthodox houses may prefer a Brāhmaṇ woman to assist at all *strī ācār*s, but there are no set rules for this. Some *strī ācār*s follow shortly after the completion of stages in the Brahmanic rituals, and both are often performed in the same place.

What then is the meaning of these *strī ācār*s to the women who perform them? Why do women perform them as a group? What do they contribute to our understanding of Bengali society and ritual symbolism in general? What do the variations according to occasion and group mean? What do they have to do with marriage and caste? To answer these questions, I had to observe what category of person performs what act; in relation to what object, act, or other person; and in what context. This led me naturally to a consideration of women as a totality of living reality in everyday life as well as in ritual and in other more specific domains of action.

*Strī ācār*s are handed down to daughters and wives of the line by the elder women of the *baṇgśa* and *ghar*. The rites performed in the *śvaśur bāṛi* can differ markedly from those of the *bāper bāṛi,* thus reflecting the difference between the lines in a marriage alliance. Since a woman adopts her husband's *niyam karan* (code for conduct) after marriage, she has to learn the way *strī ācār*s are performed in her new house. She learns as the life cycle or daily rituals occur, instructed by teachers who themselves were from different lines, once alien to the ways of the performance. Many rites are a part of the oral tradition of the house, although the manuscript version of a performance initiated by an ancestor may be a household treasure. Additions to or discontinuations of a practice are handed down orally. Unlike *brata*s (rites for the deities of the line), the *strī ācār*s of the line are not printed in pamphlet or book form, nor are they ever circulated. *Brata*s and *pañcali*s (songs) are specific to certain deities or even temples, whereas *strī ācār*s are specific to lines alone. Unlike the Brahmanic rituals (*pūjā*s), the *strī ācār*s do not include *mantra*s (incantations) set down in the sacred texts, though they do include recitations spoken as the performance goes on.

Certain rites may be dropped because of an accident or other inauspicious occurrence either following or during the performance. Failure to do the ritual properly may have the effect of a *badha* (bad omen). Such a *badha* is enough to discontinue a ritual, since it is believed that future performance would be followed by similar bad results: death, misfortune, accident, ill luck, or trouble for the house and anyone related to the line. Experience determines whether *strī ācār*s are kept or discontinued. They are supposed to achieve a desired good result, and they are honored according to the record of their work.[1] The deities involved in these *badha* rites are not discarded with the rite; instead they are worshipped in other contexts.

The representations of the gods in the *ācār*s differ from those in Sanscritized rites. The women do not use the images of the gods associated with Brahmanic temple worship. Sometimes no object stands for the gods; other times divinities are represented by a pot of rice (Lakṣmī), a grinding stone (Ṣaṣṭhī), or other items of daily use sacred to the gods. Human beings can also represent the gods, the bride being Lakṣmī or Sitā and the groom being Nārāyan. Unlike the *brata*s, which are performed for specific favors or boons already granted or expected to be granted, women perform *ācār*s seeking the blessings of the gods without expecting specific returns, with the understanding that they themselves, married women, have blessings to impart. Marriage *ācār*s exhibit the richness and beauty as well as the discipline of the new world the couple will enter.

The survival of the male line and its safe continuation are the central concerns of women's rituals. As stated before, the continuation of the line is related to everyday life (*saṇgsār*) as well as to the conception of the person and other central symbols. Here, one can begin to grasp the importance of the rituals to women since these are the celebrations of femaleness, marriedness, and motherhood for the participants themselves. In addition, the rites are meant to ensure the auspicious and harmonious life of house and line.[2] The rites reflect the practical concerns of women yet are related to Hindu ideologies in general (without the cosmic and abstract concerns of much sectarian Hindu thought).

Women and the Brāhmaṇ Priest as Ritualists

*Strī ācār*s can be contrasted directly with Brahmanical rituals: the latter follow textual rules; the former are part of everyday life, exhibiting a concern with *saṇgsār*.[3] The Brāhmaṇ priest is the main ritualist in the Sanskritic rites of marriage. These rites are in full accord with the sacred texts (Śāstras) and rules of Brahmanic ritual in general. On the other hand, the priest has no part in the *strī ācār*s even though these also involve the deities of the Hindu pantheon. In these rituals women act as Brāhmaṇs in relation to bride and groom, to sacred and other objects, to the marriage itself, and to all other participants.

The most important Brahmanic rites are the worship of the ancestors, *nāndīmukh*; the invocation of Lord Kuber (treasurer of the gods) and the Goddess of Wealth, the *basu dhārā*; and the high point of the marriage ceremonies, *sampradān,* wherein the bride's father gives his daughter to the groom amid many incantations and offerings to the gods. *Sampradān* includes the Seven Steps of Marriage and the *āgni sakkhī* (fire ritual). Brāhmaṇ-caste marriages are different from those of other castes in that there are more rituals, especially those performed the day after *sampradān.*

In the *nāndīmukh,* the rite honoring the ancestors, the Brāhmaṇ invokes Ṣaṣṭhī/Markandiya into the *ghat,* a clay vessel filled with water. Water is sacred—the means by which gods arrive into and depart from the human world. Images and other objects of the gods are immersed in water once they are no longer needed. Kuber and Lakṣmī are invoked in *basu dhārā,* a ritual drawing put on the wall of the house with oil, turmeric, vermilion, a piece of cloth, and cowries stuck on with cow dung mixed with earth. In all these rites women assist the priest. The Brāhmaṇ is in a state of purity, so no one may touch him while he performs the rites. Together with the gods, the ancestors and the personal or incarnate god Nārāyan are invoked, brought to witness the marriage, and honored. The house-

Basu dhārā: ritual drawing on wall commemorating an auspicious occasion.

hold divinities, the *kuladebatā* (god of the line), and the fire (*āgni sakkhī*, literally, "fire witness") are all worshipped by the Brāhmaṇ.[4] Each divinity has a special function at a specific stage of the marriage rituals.

Women's rituals are not the polar opposites of these Brahmanic rites. Both express the same principles of purity and pollution, levels

Nāndīmukh: ritual honoring one's ancestors.

of divinity, and relations between men and gods. The Brāhmaṇ is the model for the women's ritual action because only Brāhmaṇs can offer sacrifice (via *pūjā* and *homa*) to the gods. The purity (*śuddhatā*) of the Brāhmaṇ allows him to offer *pūjā* to the gods on behalf of other worshippers. In relation to the gods the Brāhmaṇ is hierarchically superior to all other castes. His special powers and duty (*dharmaśakti*) allow him to bring the gods to men. In the context of sacred rituals (*dharmanusṭhān*), the Brāhmaṇ, using sacred objects and uttering sacred incantations (*mantras*), invokes the gods into clay images (*murtis*), paintings (*paṭs*), or *ghats*. Giving life (*prān-pratiśṭhā*) to these inanimate objects, he makes the gods appear and partake of the offerings.[5]

Women in a *strī ācār* take on a role functionally equivalent to that of the Brāhmaṇ in a *pūjā*. Women perform similar acts, their *dharmaśakti* being their married state and status, itself a sacred object in the rituals and the subject for celebrating the young couple. The Brāhmaṇ is a ritualist by virtue of his purity and position in caste hierarchy; women are ritualists in the same manner, performing the same acts, because of the meaning of marriage in Bengali life. Just as the Brāhmaṇ invokes the gods in a *pūjā,* so too do the women invoke the goddess in the bride and divinize bride and groom as a combined male/female category, expressing a basic complementarity in Bengali society. Women do this in accordance with the sacredness of marriage and the central role of the married woman in the *saṇgsār* of caste, kinship, and household.

Women and the Brāhmaṇ priest are ritualists in different contexts. When the one is the chief ritualist, the other is absent or subordinate. Women prepare and fry *khoi* (pulses), which is in turn purified and used in the ritual by the Brāhmaṇ priest. The Brāhmaṇ is intermediary between men and gods on all occasions. In this sense, women *are* Brāhmaṇs in *strī ācār*s. Otherwise, women are goddesses and wealth in their own marriage rituals. Furthermore, Lord Kuber and Lakṣmī are husband and wife in relation to symbols of wealth. During other life cycle rituals there are different husband/wife pairs of gods. In these rituals, women are often associated with one or another goddess in relation to an object or food representing the male divinity.

The *Strī Ācār*s of Marriage

The *strī ācār*s of marriage are divided into three groups. First, there are the rites directly involving deities. These are performed to ask the gods for *maṅgal kāmonā* for the young couple. Next come the rites performed by married women for the auspicious life of the bride and groom together. The last group of rites concerns the bride and groom directly. Here, the women treat the couple as a divine pair to be served by a series of symbolic actions. This set of rites composes the welcome and farewell rituals wherein both bride and groom are gods arriving and departing.

Various marriage *strī ācār*s come before, after, or during the other marriage rites. First is *khoi bhaja* (frying the pulses). Five or seven women fry pulses to be used a day or two later in the marriage ceremonies. Then come the rites of *śaṅkha paṛāna,* the wearing of the conch-shell bangles. The bride's father provides a pair of bangles, which are put on her wrists by a Śaṅkari (shell-maker). According to the myths of the ritual, the Goddess Durgā, mother of all Bengalis, went to her in-laws' house (that of Lord Śiva, her husband). There she was made fun of for not having jewelry on her arms. Returning to the house of her father, King Dasaratha, she was met by Śiva disguised as a Śaṅkari who offered her shell bangles to propitiate her anger. Since then all brides wear conch-shell bangles as a sign of marriage. Besides being one of the attributes of Lakṣmī, the shell is sacred in many other contexts. Next, the *gāe halud strī ācār* (rite of splashing turmeric on the bride or groom) is performed. Here, the items of the ritual—especially turmeric—have particular meanings, in sacred and in everyday contexts. Soon after this *kalāi mugla* is performed. This rite (as noted in Chapter 2) is a celebration of the Goddess of Children and the *śil noṛā* (grinding stone and pestle). Following this, the cowrie games of women, *kauṛe khelā,* are performed. Besides being a symbol of Lakṣmī, cowries symbolize wealth in terms of money and children.

Special bathing rites before, during, and after marriage ceremonies also form a part of the marriage *strī ācār*s. The various purificatory rites express stages in the preparation of the bride and groom for *saṇgsār* and marriage, the women making the bride and groom fit to enter and experience the next stage. Some of these are recorded in the myths of the Snake Goddess Manasā (especially the bathing on the *śil noṛā*) and in those of Ṣaṣṭhī. (The two goddesses are related in other contexts as well, for according to the women's cultural and local conception, the protective and destructive powers of Manasā and Ṣaṣṭhī are complementary.) Finally, the welcoming and farewell rites complete the list of the marriage *strī ācār*s; these rites are particularly important ones because so many of women's symbols in Bengali society are defined, expressed, and made meaningful in them.

Once the date of the marriage is determined, the women of the household make arrangements for the performance of the *strī ācār*s. In addition to women of the house, relatives, neighbors, and caste sisters in a close relationship to the house may be invited. Excepting those in a *jajmani* relationship, lower caste women are usually not asked to come. Women in a *jajmani* relationship are, however, involved in the performance of the rituals; their blessings (*maṅgal kāmonā*) are solicited for the bride and groom. Most of the women are related (*āttiya*), and the rest are from higher castes. The Nāpit (barber) woman who attends the *kāmāno* rites is asked to invite selected women to the *strī ācār*s. Each woman will have to go through the purificatory rites. Making her visits, the Nāpit offers each woman *pān* and *supari* (betel nut), items auspicious and necessary for most rituals. The women usually know if they are expected, yet they wait for the Nāpit to come and invite them.

Āttiya living in the same house need not be issued invitations. Formal invitations are necessary in cases where the residents of the house are divided in terms of inheritance and ancestral property. A concerted effort is made to invite all relatives with whom quarrels or disputes have severed the *āttiya* tie. Such "cut-off" relatives may not attend, but they are asked anyway because of the auspicious nature of the occasion. Those who come to a marriage feast are not merely guests; they are also the bearers of blessings for the young couple. It is especially meaningful when the guest is also a *kuṭum* or *āttiya*. Women coming for the *strī ācār*s offer the auspiciousness and blessings of their married status to the bride and groom. For this, they are offered *paona*s in return: purity, merit from the rituals, pure food, and auspiciousness for helping to establish a new line.

The Symbolism of Food

Khoi bhaja, the frying of the pulses, must be done the day before marriage because on the day itself Ṣaṣṭhī/Markandiya is worshipped and pulses cannot be fried that day. Thursdays are also forbidden days because they are sacred to Lakṣmī, who is worshipped on the day of marriage. The women invited for the *strī ācār*s gather separately in the houses of bride and groom. Five, seven, or nine women participate, depending on the number of days the house observes the birth pollution rules. The pulses are fried on clean, wet sand in a metal pan. Since the gods are going to be invoked in the fried pulses, no oil can be used, so the food will be pure. The women stand in a circle holding each other by the shoulders while the *ginnī* slowly turns over the pulses and sand with a bunch of twigs. Only a small amount is fried at a time, and the *khoi* is collected in a bamboo basket. The process is repeated five, seven, or nine times. The women are given a betel nut and a *pān* as a *paona* for their services. Sweets may also be given.

Khoi is used in a number of *strī ācār*s. On the day of the marriage the *Kubi pātā* (the image of Lord Kuber, keeper of wealth, to whom daily offerings are made during the marriage ceremonies) is set up in the houses of the bride and of the groom. The altar contains three metal glasses filled with paddy (*dhān*), fried pulses (*khoi*), and crushed rice. *Khoi* is also needed for the *āgni sakkhī* (performed at the girl's house), when bride and groom pour fried pulses into the sacrificial fire (*homa*). The groom's side must bring their own fried *khoi* for the *āgni sakkhī.* In the sacred fire the *khoi* becomes an offering to

Khoi bhaja: the frying of the pulses.

the Lord Viṣṇu, the maintainer of the universe, who becomes a witness of the marriage rituals and confers his blessings upon the couple.

All the articles for the *homa* have to be brought by the groom's side. If any item, including the *khoi*, is forgotten, the groom's people have to purchase it from the bride's house, and in this case a high price is charged. The *homa* ritual is performed at a stage in the marriage when the virgin is "made into a wife." It is for this reason that all the items used must come from the groom's side. At this moment, gods, ancestors, relatives, and other guests are asked to witness the transformation about to take place. The bride now becomes a full-fledged member of the groom's house.

What is accomplished by women, given the fact that it is the Brāhmaṇ who has to perform the *homa* ritual as well as the *pūjā* of Lord Kuber (the two rites where *khoi* is particularly significant)? Women and priest share the rituals of Lord Kuber. Women partici-

Agni sakkhī: ritual offering to the sacrificial fire (*homa*), the witness of the marriage.

pate in the *pūjā* by setting up the *Kubi pātā* and preparing the *khoi* offering. The women pray for wealth (goods and children) to remain in the house. In both *Kubi pūjā* and *homa*, *khoi* and women are related to notions of wealth. In turn, women and wealth become sacred in the performance of the rituals.

Wearing the Conch-shell Bangles

The first *strī ācār* on the day of the marriage is *śaṅkha poṛāna,* when the bride is made to wear the conch-shell bangles given by her father. This rite is not performed in the groom's house and the groom does not give conch-shell bangles. An important parallel ritual is performed in the groom's house on the fourth day after the marriage, when the groom gives his bride an iron bangle. Iron bangles are auspicious objects, and one worn on the arm of a woman signifies that she has a living husband. A widow has to break her iron bangle on the death of her husband.

The Śaṅkari (a man of the conch-shell-maker *jāti*) is called to the bride's house early on the day of the marriage. He brings several pairs of bangles and helps the bride put them on. Because the bangles are difficult to put on, the Śaṅkari, even if he is of a lower caste, is allowed to touch the bride. He must be careful not to break the bangles, for that would mean bad luck, an inauspicious beginning for the bride.[6]

Early in the morning the bride bathes, changes into a new *sāri,* and is brought out to sit facing the Śaṅkari. The *ginnīmā* puts out a metal plate containing turmeric in water and sacred grass (*durbā*—strong, long, and straight bladed), two items used in Brahmanic rites. The Śaṅkari tries a few pairs of bangles on the bride's arm, and when a suitable pair is found it is dipped in the turmeric water for purification.[7] The first set of bangles is always bigger than the bride's hand so that she can put them on without breaking them. This pair of bangles is given to her by her father or guardian and must be preserved for one year.[8] After the bangles are selected, the Śaṅkari is given the amount of money he demands; the bride's father will not argue about the price on this day since he (like the father of Durgā) cannot give his daughter away with bare arms. The Śaṅkari is obviously going to use the occasion to demand more money than the worth of the bangles. Besides the cost of the bangles, the Śaṅkari is given a *paona* consisting of one *pāi* (a cup) of rice and some money (*dakkhina*). *Paona*s always accompany women's rituals. Finally, the mistress of the house does *praṇām* to the Śaṅkari.

Unmarried girls and children may also wear shells; it is for this reason that the father of a bride may give conch shells.[9] What he cannot give his daughter are the symbols of a married woman, iron bangles with or without the vermilion on them. Married women are never seen with bare arms; even the poor wear inexpensive plastic bangles with their iron bangle. Unlike the iron bangle and vermilion, conch-shell bangles in themselves are not truly symbolic of marriage. Both married and unmarried women can wear them, although older, unmarried girls may wear conch-shell bangles only with the permission of the *ginnī* and the other female members of the house. Unmarried girls may wear one conch-shell bangle, but married women may wear these bangles only in pairs.

A father may also give his unmarried daughters *sāri*s and conch-shell bangles, the combination of the two known as *śaṅkha sāri.* The former can also be gifts from a brother to his unmarried sisters. In contrast, *āltā sāri,* a *sāri* along with a lac-dye mixture used to color the feet of women, is a type of gift usually given to married women by their husbands. Iron bangles, *āltā,* vermilion, and clothes (*praṇāmi kapar*) all celebrate the marriage. The iron bangle, the conch bangles, vermilion in the hair parting, and *āltā* worn on the feet, when used together, represent a married woman whose husband is alive. If the conch shells are worn separately without the iron bangle, or the *āltā* without the vermilion, then the objects express a different meaning to those beholding them.

Smearing Turmeric on Bride and Groom

Gāe halud (turmeric-on-the-body) is an auspicious ritual on the day of the marriage. Whereas before the change of the bride's *gotra,* the gift exchanges between the two houses establish the *kuṭum* tie, the *gāe halud* ritual introduces two houses to each other's *saṇgsár* in a ritual context. Whereas the giving of gifts establishes a kinship relationship, the *gāe halud* expresses marriage, married life, and the married status of women. Hence it is an important ritual.

Gāe halud is performed in the houses of both bride and groom, although it cannot be performed at both houses simultaneously because the turmeric for the bride's *gāe halud* must come from the groom's house after the rite has been performed there. The time of performance is fixed in the *pañjikā* (calendar, which gives the dates and times of day for the performance of many rituals associated with marriage) according to the astrologically calculated most auspicious moment. The groom's side notifies the bride's house when its *gāe halud* will be performed since the bride's *gāe halud* cannot begin before the groom's. Where distance is no problem, several people from the groom's house take some of the turmeric-and-water mixture with which the ritual was performed and bring it, together with the *gāe halud tattva,* in procession to the bride's house.

Lack of transportation and distance may prevent the groom's house from sending the turmeric and *gāe halud tattva* to the bride's in

Gāe halud: smearing turmeric paste on the bride's chest.

Items used for *gāe halud*.

time, for if *gāe halud* cannot be performed within the astrologically given time (*lagna*) the whole ritual becomes inauspicious. Hence, in many cases the bride's house proceeds with its performance, using its own turmeric, before the groom's *tattva*s arrive. Then, when the turmeric from the groom's house does arrive, a second, less elaborate *gāe halud* is performed, using a mixture of turmeric from the groom's and the bride's houses. The *gāe halud* exchanges of turmeric and the gifts from the groom's side are the first set of things exchanged by bride and groom and the first gifts made during the marriage by one house to the other.

When the procession with the *gāe halud tattva* arrives at the bride's house, the women blow on conch shells or take up the *ululu* (an auspicious cadence women utter at the time of *strī ācār*s). The party from the groom's house is welcomed, invited inside, and feasted. The bride is dressed in her *gāe halud sāri* (which she must keep for one year) and is brought out to the *camlatalā* (the enclosure where the rituals are performed) by the women.[10] Gifts are spread out for all to see. The *ginnīmā* (the eldest woman of the house or the bride's mother or a Brāhmaṇ woman in the case of a non-Brāhmaṇ house) covers the bride's head with the end part (*ācal*) of the *sāri* and makes her sit next to the *camlatalā*. The bride sits on a *piṛi*, a low stool decorated with rice-paste drawings representing Lakṣmī and her attributes. This is the same *piṛi* she will sit on later at night while she is carried by the men of the house out to the *camlatalā* and around the groom seven times. Now the *uttān talā*, the plate containing 27 auspicious items (all sacred and all used in other life cycle rituals and temple *pūjā*s as well), is placed in front of the bride.

The *ginnī* begins the ritual by taking a red thread from the *uttān talā* and tying it around the bride's waist. Next, she puts a *bel mala* (a garland of sacred wood-apple) around the bride's neck. The *nitkanyā* (a prepubertal girl who accompanies the bride during most rituals) sits next to the bride and has red thread and *bel mala* put on her as well, for everything done to the bride is also done to the *nitkanyā*. The *ginnī* then takes some turmeric paste and coconut oil and applies them one at a time to the bride's forehead, neck, chest, shoulders, and arms. The paste and oil are used liberally and rubbed in thoroughly. Oil is rubbed on the bride's hair. The *ginnī* next takes a wooden comb from the *uttān talā* and, letting the bride see herself, asks if she is pleased with the performance. The bride is grateful for the ritual and does *praṇām* to the *ginnī* in humility. Now the five, seven, or nine women each repeat the whole performance, after which the bride does *praṇām* to each. The *nitkanyā* is similarly served, after which she too must do obeisance. The ritual is considered to be significant and auspicious: the bride will soon be a wife (*strī*) just like the women who perform the ritual. Later, the five, seven, or nine women of the *strī ācār*s hold each other's hands and jointly give the bride the *kājal latā,* a small iron object in which collyrium is kept.[11] The bride is asked to keep this object for at least eight days, until the *aṣṭamaṅgala,* after which she can give it to her unmarried *nanod* (HZ).

The turmeric-smearing rite completed, the bride's head is covered and she is taken into the *Kubi ghar* to worship Lord Kuber. The bride's face is uncovered after she has done *praṇām* to Lord Kuber. Each ritual during the marriage ceremonies ends in the *Kubi ghar.* Here, too, the women are ritualists, since Kuber is the treasurer of the gods and represents the wealth of women (wealth as goods and as children of the line). Once the *Kubi pūjā* is performed, the bride may roam around the house but is not allowed to go outside without being accompanied by other women. For eight days she is not supposed to let go of the *kājal latā.*[12]

The same rituals are observed in the groom's house, where married women smear turmeric and oil on the groom.[13] But instead of a *kājal latā* the groom is given a betel-nut cutter to hold. Here again, the complementary symbolism of male and female is striking. The cutter, parallel in symbolism to the collyrium holder, relates to birth rituals where the umbilical cord is cut, severing the *phol* (fruit) from its container (womb, mother), allowing the father to introduce the child into the world as a carrier of his line. Both bride and groom hold on to the *kājal latā* and cutter, respectively, until the marriage rites are completed. The giving of these iron objects forms an integral part of the *strī ācār* in the *gāe halud.*

The bride and the women cry throughout the performance, for soon the bride will have to leave the house of her girlhood. *Gāe halud* is a rite of sorrow as well as happiness. There is much joy when a girl fulfills an ideal of womanhood by receiving a husband. But there is sadness at the imminent departure of the bride from her father's house and sorrow for the anticipated tribulations of the bride's new life.

The observance of *gāe halud ācār* may vary in detail from caste to caste, but despite these differences, the overall meaning of the rituals is the same. The variations are not in the actual performance and participation, which are similar among all the different castes, including the Muslims. The differences lie in whether or not the bride's mother covers her daughter's head with the *ācal* of her *sāri* and whether or not she holds a *kulo* (a flat bamboo basket used for winnowing) over her head. Both *ācal* and *kulo* are auspicious (and in this context, sacred) items used to protect the bride from evil or bad influence that someone might wish to impart to her. By using the *ācal* of her *sāri*, the mother takes evil or inauspicious happening upon herself. The *kulo* has several auspicious signs on it, and a piece of red cloth, a banana, and a flower are placed upon it. The items are offerings to the "auspiciousness and blessings of the gods," which the mother and many other women desire to bestow on bride and groom.

Regardless of variations, the turmeric-smearing rituals are in general simple and short: together women attempt to help the bride and groom into a new phase of life and a new status by reenacting the making of a marriage, reinstating their married status, contrasting themselves to widows and unmarried women (*abibāhita meye*), and contrasting their sexually active lives (in terms of producing children) with the barrenness of a widow's life (being unable to bear children). The *gāe halud strī ācār* is for the women the functional equivalent of the Brahmanic *gotra badal* (exchange) ritual. In this rite, performed later at night, the bride changes her *gotra* and is adopted by the groom's people (*gotra, bhāiyat,* and *baṇgśa*). For the women, the turmeric-smearing ritual is equally important and necessary; in *gāe halud* they stand in the same relation to the bride, the sacred, and the gods as does the Brāhmaṇ in the major *pūjā*s and Brahmanic rituals of marriage.

Married women reenact their own passage from virginity and their father's house to conjugal life in the father-in-law's house. The *gāe halud strī ācār* established the married state for the bride by accepting her into the society of *strī lok*. For the women performing this *strī ācār*, this is a way of defining their domain of action, establishing their role in the sacred scheme. It is also a way of complementing male roles in ritual, in marriage, in conception, and in the *saṇgsār*. It prepares a woman for and fulfills her contribution to the creation, maintenance, and transmission of lives. Throughout the ritual the women treat the bride as a divinity, they themselves being Lakṣmī and Ṣaṣṭhī. Just as the Brāhmaṇ becomes a god serving gods, so do the women in their sacred roles serve a goddess who will soon become a wife and mother. All these are in fact the same actions the Brāhmaṇ performs when he gives life and respectful service to the clay image of a divinity.

Mixing Oil and Pulses

The *strī ācār* following *gāe halud* is *kalāi mugla*, the mixture of oil and pulses described and analyzed in Chapter 2, with emphasis there on the exchange aspect of the ritual. The symbolism of *śil noṛā* in relation to the Goddess Ṣaṣṭhī and her consort, and the significant parallel between *kalāi mugla* and the first menstruation rites were also discussed there.[14] Let me briefly redescribe the ritual in the context of women as ritualists.

In the *kalāi mugla* the bride and groom (in their separate houses) stand for *śil noṛā,* male/female, and Ṣaṣṭhī/Markandiya. After a *pān* is pressed to the bride's or groom's forehead, women pour oil on it, which drips down onto the bound hands of bride or groom, each of whom is then told by the women to mix the pulses well. Here the male/female complementarity in marriage, conception, and birth is explicitly expressed. Bride and groom separately enact the union of male and female, and the basic complementarity that encompasses all persons, men and women alike. In this ritual the person about to be married stands for the complementary pair. In addition bride and groom stand for the divine figures of the goddess and her lord, both sets of meanings being accomplished in relation to the potential creation of children in marriage.

Playing with Cowries

Cowries, which play a part in most temple and *strī ācār* rituals, are associated with the Goddess Lakṣmī.[15] The cowrie games, *kauṛe khelā,* are neither played in all marriages nor necessarily observed in both the bride's and the groom's houses. In some cases they are separately performed immediately after *gāe halud* in both houses; in others they are played on *kāl rātri* (the day after the marriage) in the groom's house. The games do not contribute to the development and building up of ritual action in the marriage ceremonies, though they do symbolize certain accomplishments up to a particular stage. The games are of two kinds: those played by the married women with bride or groom and those played by the new *swāmī strī* (husband and wife), either in the *bāsar ghar* (the room in the bride's house where the bride and groom stay up all night after the completion of the marriage) or in the groom's house soon after the welcoming rituals.

Seniority and sex are not barriers in the games since all the males present in the house are included: *āttiya jāmāi, jñati,* and also *kuṭum,* most of whom attend the night festivities. Men, even one's HB (with whom an avoidance relationship is normally observed) participate. The women do, however, exclude unmarried girls and widows from the games since neither can participate in *gāe halud.* This is a time of mirth and joy among all the married women, a time of bantering

Kauṛe khelā: married woman prepares the *kol sara* for the cowrie game.

and much lewd joking, light irreverence, laughing, and a lot of running around. Amid much teasing and sexual joking, they apply colored water, oil and colored powder, turmeric and water to each other. One is reminded of the festival of color and role reversal at the time of *Holi* (Marriott, 1966). At the end, sweets, *pān*, and *supari* are distributed to all participants.

At the marriage rituals, cowries represent the deity of wealth and children (*santān*). The *kauṛe khelā* played by the married women uses as many cowries as the number of children the participating women wish the young couple to have. The five, seven, or nine women sit together in a circle, a canopy held over their heads. If the games are played in both houses after *gāe hālud*, bride and groom are each made to sit in the circle. It is more usual, however, for the games to be played with the groom alone.

Before the games actually start, one of the women takes a flat clay pot from the *camlatalā* and puts nine cowries, nine betel nuts, nine cardamom seeds, and nine whole turmeric roots into it. Another clay pot is used to cover the assemblage, and the two are tied together to make the *kol sara*. The women then place the *kol sara* on the *śil* propped up by the *noṛā*. The groom is then invited to break the *kol sara* with his left foot. The women then count the broken pot sherds, for the number of pieces indicates the number of children the couple will have. The cowries, seeds, and roots are collected again, and the games are begun.

The elder married sister of the groom starts by tossing up the cowries and seeds three times in her cupped hands. Without dropping any, she passes the assemblage to the next woman in the circle, who repeats the procedure and in turn passes the cowries and seeds to the next woman. This is continued until all the women in the circle have played and the groom is reached. The groom throws the cowries three times, and when he is done his sister ties up the collection in a piece of cloth died yellow with turmeric. This small bundle is known as *girt chāṛā,* and its ends are used to tie together the clothes of bride and groom during the ritual at night when the vermilion is put into the parting of the bride's hair. The *girt chāṛā* is another item that has to be brought to the bride's house by the groom's party. If it is forgotten, the groom has to purchase the *girt chāṛā* of the bride's house.

In the *kauṛe khelā* played by the *swāmī strī,* a *pāi* (measuring cup) of paddy is given to bride and groom together with a few cowries. The groom pours out the rice and the bride fills the *pāi* again. This is repeated five, seven, or nine times, and then the bride spills the *pāi* and the groom collects the rice. Later, the groom throws five, seven, or nine cowries and the bride gathers them up. Then the spilling and collecting is reversed again. Finally, the bride holds a full *pāi* of paddy on her head and walks with the groom to the *ṭhākur ghar* (the worship room where the gods of the house are kept) or to the rice storage room. While walking, the groom keeps throwing paddy from the *pāi* with the aid of small twigs. Reaching the room, both do *praṇām* to the gods or the paddy jars, after which the bride collects all the rice spilled on the way with the help of the same twigs used by the groom.

The *pāi* of paddy when filled to the brim represents the Goddess Lakṣmī; cowries in a pot may also represent her. The *Lakkhi saj,* the altar of Lakṣmī, consists of a *pāi* filled with paddy, a bowl of cowries, an anthropomorphic metal image of the goddess (though this is not necessary), and a few animal figures made of brass—all signs of Lakṣmī. But paddy and cowries are enough to represent the deity, and in the *strī ācār* no other images are used. Brahmanic temple rituals often require *Lakkhi saj,* as in the great festival of the Goddess Durgā. Paddy represents wealth as well as sacredness.

Wealth, *dhan,* is related to paddy, *dhān.* In playing with paddy and cowries, married women symbolize what they themselves mean to

Bride and groom in front of *camlatalā* filling and emptying the *pāi* (a rice measurement) with unhusked rice.

the houses of their fathers-in-law. Just as the objects express the wealth of the house, so too are women wealth to their *śvaśur ghar*. For women, the married status is equivalent to the Goddess Lakṣmī in combination with the Goddess Ṣaṣṭhī. The attributes of these two deities are alternately represented in the *strī ācār*s at marriage. Either it is wealth or property or the bride as a goddess that is being identified with Lakṣmī; or it is the possession of the children, living husband, and women as divine mothers that is being identified with Ṣaṣṭhī. The interplay and alternation between two sets of symbols and two sets of attributes manifesting two different deities expresses the dual meaning of married status for women and the position of a woman between two houses and two *baṇgśa*s. The deities are kept separate in other rituals, but in the marriage *strī ācār*s they are merged because it is here that the notion of the married woman is generated and constructed. The symbolism of the two goddesses is independently recognizable. In other rituals the attributes specify one goddess or the other (being aspects of the same thing, when one is present, the other is absent), but in marriage the two are brought together. Children, wealth, femaleness, married state, and lineality originate here. A woman is her husband's wealth and the transmitter of his line. Women grant to the line children, who in turn bring further wealth to the house. At the moment of marriage, a woman encompasses the attributes of Lakṣmī *and* Ṣaṣṭhī.[16]

The Bathing Rituals

There are three main bathing (*snān*) rituals in a Bengali marriage. The first takes place on the afternoon of the marriage, when the bride and groom, still in their respective houses, are taken in procession to the local ponds. Either Doms (drum players) playing the *ḍhol* or a party of musicians head the procession of bride or groom and their party of women. Friends, neighbors, and children bring up the rear of the festive crowd. Women blow conch shells and cry their auspicious *ululu*. Today it is becoming fashionable to go to the pond in rickshaws or even cars. From this point until the marriage is over, bride and groom must fast.

At the pond, the five, seven, or nine women hold the groom or bride by the hand—the same actions being repeated in both houses—and lead him or her to the edge of the water. The groom with his betel-nut cutter and the bride with her *kājal latā* each draw a square in the water to represent a room and stand in the center of it. Water removes pollution and the square serves to confine bride or groom (who are in a pure, therefore vulnerable, state) to a sacred (*pabittra*) area where evil spirits may not trespass.

As the square is drawn on the surface of the water, one of the women throws a betel nut and a *pān* into the center as a *paona* to the spirits (both evil and benign) and to the water itself. Only then is the groom or the bride ready to take the bath. Standing in the center, each of the women sprinkles water on the groom or bride; some may smear turmeric and oil on the bride's body and hair. After this, the bride (and groom separately in his house) are left to take a bath by themselves but they may not leave the drawn square. Once they are finished, they take a final purifying dip in the water by completely immersing themselves. When they emerge, their faces are covered with a *pān*. Assisted by the women, they walk home with their faces covered, to be uncovered only after each has paid respect to Lord Kuber. After this the groom and bride prepare themselves for the evening rituals of the marriage, and the women of the bride's house arrange and prepare the house for the welcome of the groom and his party (*bār jātri*).

The bathing rituals are performed in various ways, and I found that not all castes in Vishnupur follow the same way. Having bathed, the bride is assisted by her mother or sister to the edge of the pond (*ghāt*), where a few more rituals may be performed before the bride walks home. The plate containing the 27 sacred and auspicious items (*uttān talā*) is brought to the *ghāt*. The *ginnīmā* takes some mud from the pond and places it on the stairs of the *ghāt* leading to the water. The *kājal latā* is taken from the *uttān talā*, held to the bride's forehead, and then inserted into the pile of mud standing upright. Flowers from the *uttān talā* are then touched to the bride's forehead and thrown onto the *kājal latā*. The same process is repeated with honey, curds, paddy, and grass. Once this is over, the bride is assisted by other women to do *praṇām* (with face covered) to the *ginnīmā*. The *ginnīmā* finally removes the *kājal latā*, throwing the mud into the pond. She then washes the ritual area before returning home.

In this rite, Lord Śiva is represented by the *kājal latā*; the performance is similar to that offered to *Śiva liṅga*. Not only is the *kājal latā* like Śiva's *liṅga* (male symbol) but the pile of mud is like Durgā's *yoni* (female symbol). The symbolism of Śiva/Durgā, male and female, is clear and significant. The Sanskrit term *yoni* also means "place or element of birth." The *yoni* expresses *bhaga* (enjoyment, acceptance) of the *liṅga bīj* (seed). The *liṅga* and *yoni* together "is a cosmic philosophy based on the union of the sexes" (Balfour, 1885, 3: 1117).

Snān: first ritual bathing of the bride.

The symbolism of the male and female principles is also demonstrated in the rituals. According to the women, the *yoni* stands for femaleness, the female principle in the complementarity of *puruṣ/prakriti*. The *yoni* is complemented by the *liṅga*, and the two together, the *liṅga* within the *yoni*, represents the creative process: energy, power, and action. The two together are also the standard representation of Śiva/Durgā, the male and female divinities par excellence.

The stone image of this pair as worshipped in temples consists of the upright *liṅga* with a round base, the *Durgā patra* (the vessel of Durgā). The *liṅga,* a round conical stone standing perpendicularly from an oval-shaped rim cut on the same stone platform, represents the Hindu deity Śiva, who is worshipped in this form. The rim is the *yoni,* the female form. Lord Śiva worshipped in the form of *liṅga* is the regenerator; and the *yoni* (*bhaga*) is his consort, the expression of his *śakti* (power) personified as the Goddess Parvati, or Durgā. According to Hindu cosmogony in the beginning there was chaos, crude nature, *prakriti.* The male principle (*puruṣa*) had *śakti* emanate from himself.[17] In its first state, *prakriti* lay dormant and inert; then *bīja,* a vivifying principle, excited nature at rest. "This power or aptitude of nature is represented by the symbol of the *yoni* or *bhaga,* while the *bīja* or animating principle is expressed by the *liṅga*" (Balfour, 1885, 3: 1117).

In the bathing ritual the mud base for the *kājal latā* is the *yoni,* while the upright collyrium holder is the *liṅga.* The *kājal latā* is dabbed with milk, honey, coconut water, and curds (as is the *liṅga* of Śiva when worshipped in temple rituals). Unmarried girls perform Śiva *brata* in exactly the same manner, the purpose of the ritual being to secure a Śiva-like husband. But the *kājal latā* is only worshipped as *liṅga* in the bride's bathing ritual, so I conclude that, in addition to representing the union of male and female elements, this ritual (performed by the bride's mother) is also a way of announcing the maturing of the virgin's reproductive powers and a foreshadowing of her ability to create offspring in the union of marriage. Nevertheless, it is also an expression of bride and groom as a divine pair, consorts in the manner of Śiva and Durgā.

On the day after the marriage the second bathing ritual, the *śil noṛā snān,* takes place, assisted by a male Nāpit (barber). It is the first ritual the bride and groom perform together. Bride and groom wear new clothes, which become the Nāpit's *paona* after the bath. A hole is dug in the yard of the house. The *noṛā* is placed over the hole and the *śil* is laid on top of the *noṛā.* Two married women of the house each bring a *kulsi* (a large brass pitcher) of *nisi* (dawn) water taken from the pond first thing in the morning. Assisting the bride and groom throughout, the women of the *strī ācār* bring the couple out and make them stand or sit together on the *śil.* One of the women pours a *kulsi* of water into the hole under the *śil.* The Nāpit takes the thread from the *uttān talā* and walks around the couple seven times, binding them together. The *ginnīmā* picks up the *uttān talā* and does *baran* (a welcoming ritual) to the bride and groom: she touches the plate to the groom's forehead, then to the earth, and up again to the groom's head; repeats this three times; and then the bride is similarly welcomed. Some women ring bells (also used in temple rituals) and blow on conch shells, while others take up the *ululu*. The Nāpit or one of the married women sprinkles water on the couple from the second *kulsi*; only a few drops of water are needed to imply that the couple has bathed.

The services of the barber are needed in many rituals, especially to remove birth and death pollution. In marriage ritual, his services are employed to bathe the couple and remove pollution. One may understand this aspect of the Nāpit's services by looking at the myth of Manasā and Behulā. On the night of her marriage, Behulā became a widow; her husband died as a result of Manasā's vengeance. Therefore, after the marriage is performed, the couple stays up all night in the *bāsar ghar*. They are not allowed to fall asleep or leave the room together; one must always remain. The fear of death, an evil happening, or an inauspicious act remains to this day. Although the myth is acknowledged and maintained by keeping awake, no formal worship is done to the Goddess Manasā. Yet her power is acknowledged and respected in the bath the couple take together the next morning while standing on the *śil noṛā*. The *śil noṛā* represents the deity Ṣaṣṭhī (there being myths in which the manifestations of one deity or the other stand in complementary relation to each other; Manasā being, thus, one form of Ṣaṣṭhi in a particular context).

Having survived the night without any danger, the couple begs Ṣaṣṭhī to help them maintain a married life together, to grant them children, and help keep them well. One can say that bride and groom wash away the possibility of death in the ritual. In this sense the couple jointly worships the goddesses, pleading for children and protection, leaving behind them danger, impurity, and the inauspiciousness which befell Behulā. They may both stand on the *śil noṛā* without fear of what the Goddess Ṣaṣṭhī may do. This is the only context in which the *śil noṛā* can be touched by feet. On other occasions, if one's foot inadvertently touches the stones, one must do *praṇām* to the *śil noṛā* to avert inauspicious results.

Until a son or a daughter marries, he or she is a *sissu* (child) to a mother. Before the groom sets off to the marriage, his own mother washes his feet and dries them with her hair or *sāri*. The bride is similarly treated when she is welcomed into her father-in-law's house. The washing of the feet of a younger person by an older one is not an everyday occurrence. The reversal in this third bathing ritual serves to heighten the significance and sacredness of the occasion. Children are gods who are given *ādar* (love) and *sneha* (filial love). Ṣaṣṭhī is a benign mother to all children, to bride and groom, and as such she cannot harm them any more than one can harm one's own children.

Rituals of Welcome and Farewell

The welcoming rites (*abahans*) for one's newly acquired relatives parallel Brāhmaṇ priests' welcoming rituals for the gods at the beginning of major festival cycles, reflecting parallel roles of men and gods in a sacred context. The journey of a new wife and a new husband is celebrated the way deities are received on their arrival at a festival and the way the deities are allowed to return to their abode at the end. Bride and groom are each welcomed on arrival at their respective in-laws' houses. In both cases the welcoming rituals and the activities of the married women are similar. Bride and groom are welcomed as deities, just as at the time of a *pūjā* or a woman's *brata*, the deity to be invoked and worshipped is asked to come and make her or his presence felt among the devotees.

Baran karā: groom's mother welcomes bride and groom in groom's house.

When the groom arrives at the bride's house (the marriage always taking place in the bride's father's house) the women wait for the *bār jātri* (the party accompanying the groom to the marriage). As soon as it arrives, they begin the welcome ritual, *baran karā.* They blow conch shells, ring bells, and take up the *ululu.* Before the groom enters the house, the mistress of the house takes the *uttān talā* and does *abahan* by touching the plate to the groom's forehead, then to the ground, and up to the groom again. After repeating this three times, the *ginnī* gives the groom sweets to eat and sherbet to drink. Water is poured on the doorstep as the groom steps into the house. Inside, the women make him stand in front of the *camlatalā* to finish the rest of this *strī ācār.* Once the groom's party has been served light refreshments, the welcoming rituals can continue.

The remainder of the *strī ācār* precedes the actual marriage ceremony. This ritual, known as *satas kathi,* is a way of welcoming the groom and introducing him to the women of the house. The women, carrying a torch made from the stems of *pān*s and cotton soaked in oil, walk in a circle around the groom, who stands facing the *camlatalā.* After the first woman in the circle does *abahan* with the *uttān talā,* all the women go around him five, seven, or nine times with the lit *pān* stems. The women touch the ground and then the groom's forehead as they go around.[18] In some Brāhmaṇ houses, men do the *satas kathi;* but in other castes, the women do this welcome.

After the marriage the welcoming rituals extended to the bride at her in-laws' house are somewhat different. They emphasize the divinity and royalty (as Rāmā and Sitā) of bride and groom on their marriage day. They can do no harm to man or god this day, for they are without sin (*pāp*). This explains why they can step on the *śil noṛā* without offending the Goddess Ṣaṣṭhī. In the bride's welcoming ceremony the rituals stress the relationships of the bride (as a wife of the *baṇgśa*) to the in-laws and to the other women of the house. On this, her first entry into her in-laws' house, all the rooms are kept open because a deity is about to enter (this parallels what happens at *pūjā*s of Lakṣmī). There is much excitement as the women wait to see the bride who has come to stay with them. Once inside, the bride is introduced to the house as its *baṇgśer* Lakṣmī (goddess of the line). While the bride is being introduced, milk is kept boiling on the fire and is allowed to boil over, the sight symbolizing the wealth of the house.[19]

As soon as the bride and groom arrive at the groom's house, the women involved in the welcoming rituals step outside the door, and one of them pours a *kulsi* of water on the ground under the car or the rickshaw before the couple alight. This is similar to when deities, entering the temple or the house where their *pūjā* is done, have water poured in their path to settle the dust. A flat metal plate containing a mixture of lac dye and milk is brought out by the mistress or the elder woman of the house (eSW—*jā*—or HBW to the new bride). The *jā* holds the plate under the bride's feet and the latter imprints her soles on the mixture of milk and lac (just as deities at *pūjā* have their feet dyed with lac and milk). In some houses the women wash the feet of the bride with milk and *āltā* before giving sweets and sherbet to the couple. The women then hold the bride's arm and lead her into the house, where she stands in front of the *camlatalā*. The bride stands to the left of the groom, and the two are tied to each other with the *girt chāṛā* (containing cowries, turmeric, and betel nut) between them. The mistress of the house places a fish in front of the *camlatalā* (on which in turn a fish is drawn).[20] Although a fish in water is very hard to catch and moves around a lot, outside its habitat it now lies calmly on the ground. The women of the house wish that their new *boumā* become like the fish—serene and cool. As the bride enters the house, the welcome extended to her is known as *prabes karā,* meaning "to enter into," to be welcomed into the husband's house as the Goddess Kamala.

Now other rituals follow, stressing the bride's responsibilities to the *saṇgsār* and to other members of the house and establishing her position in relation to her husband's people. The bride and groom face the *camlatalā* until the women have finished the blessings of welcome. First, the mistress of the house comes in front of the couple and holds a small metal bowl of water and a piece of golden jewelry. *Sanājal,* "golden water," is placed in front of the bride, and the mother-in-law asks her to look at the water and see her face in it. This is a way of expressing respect for each other, of treating each other like gold, precious and dear, of having the *boumā* (SW) and *śāsuṛī* (HM) begin their relationship sweetly and respectfully (*sammān*). The *śāsuṛī* is unsure about the *boumā*; the bride comes from a house with which she may have had no previous relationship. Even if the houses have been known to each other before the marriage, the *śāsuṛī* knows that her new *boumā* will never replace her own daughter. Here the conflict between mother-in-law and son's wife is foreshadowed, though both wish each other well and try to start their life together without any trouble. The *ginnī* then hands the bride the fish, which has been lying on the floor. The bride holds the fish for a short time before putting it back on the floor. She feels the coolness of the fish, an attribute she too should have.[21] The bride has now established her relationship to her mother-in-law, one of obedience and respect, and from now on she will obey and follow in the footsteps of her *śāsuṛī*.

The rituals that follow establish the bride's relationship to the married and unmarried sisters of the groom. The married *nanod* (HZ) gives the bride a *kulsi* filled with water, and the bride places it on her waist, holding one arm around it. The longer she holds the heavy *kulsi,* the stronger she is deemed; this is a test of her strength and ability to work. Since she will share in the household work, her *nanod*s let her hold the pitcher for a long time. Before the *nanod*s remove the *kulsi* they ask for a small sum of money, which the groom promises to give. The money, called the *śaṅkha sāri,* is promised and given to the young girls. Next the *nanod*s ask for a gift. Once the brother has promised to grant his sisters a *paona,* they will remove the pail from the bride's hand. Here, the groom mediates between the sisters and the new wife, the roles being reversed, since both bride and groom will act as mediators in the house.

The *ginnīmā* then continues with her rites of welcome. She blesses the bride and groom by touching the auspicious *uttān talā* to their forehead, right shoulder, and left shoulder, repeating the act three times, each time stooping and touching the ground with the plate. Next she takes the bananas from the plate. After touching them to the forehead of bride and groom, she throws the fruit over them to the children.

The ritual that follows, the wearing of the iron bangles, is paralleled by the wearing of *sindūr* (vermilion) the first time.[22] In some houses people wait until *bou bhāt,* when the young wife becomes a full member of the house, to give the iron bangle. Being seated on a *piṛi,* the husband puts an iron bangle on his wife's left arm. Women blow on conch shells, ring bells, and take up the *ululu*. The new bangle must be cared for very meticulously, for it will remain with a woman throughout her married life. Should it break, its pieces have to be collected and kept or buried under the sacred tulsi tree. The tulsi, kept in the yard of every house, is a plant sacred to Viṣṇu and Nārāyan and a representation of Viṣṇu's consort. Women never refer to an iron bangle as having broken; rather, they say it "got cold" (*ṭhānḍā*)—the same way they refer to broken conch-shell bangles.

Although unmarried girls and children wear iron bangles—usually for reasons of health—after marriage the only iron bangle a woman can wear must have been bought by the in-laws and must be worn on the left arm.[23] All other iron bangles have to be thrown away. A married woman wears bangles made from other materials as well

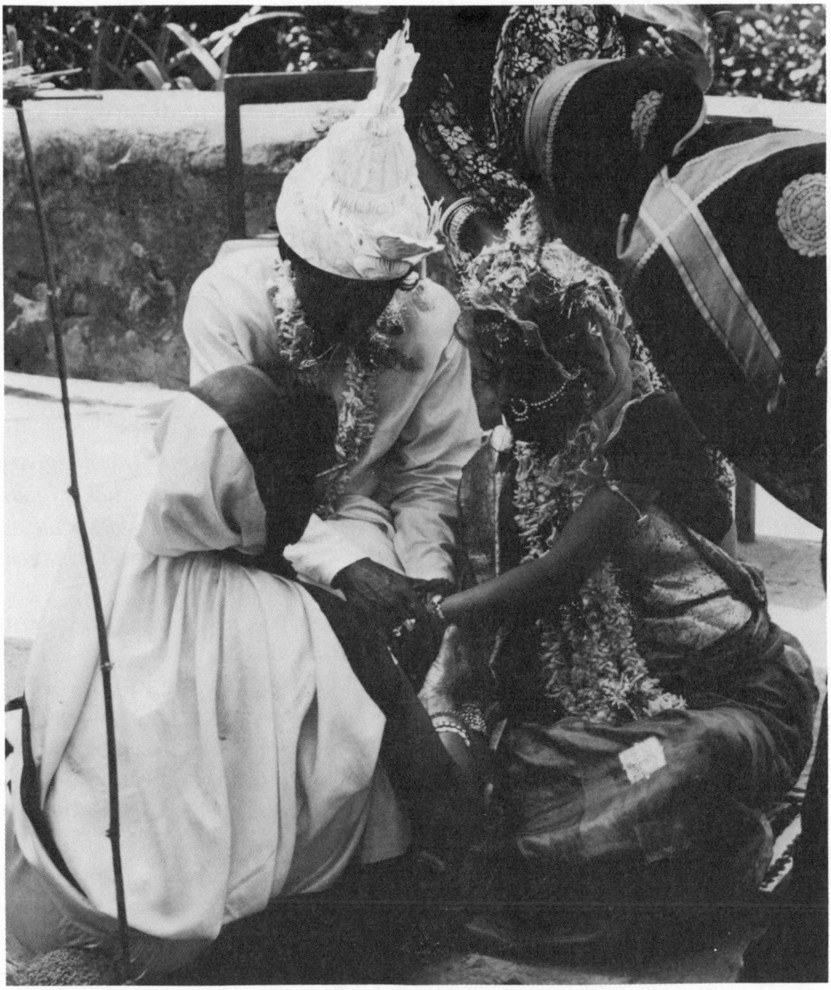

Lohā paṛāna: the husband puts an iron bangle on his wife's left arm.

(conch shells, gold, silver, glass, and plastic), yet the iron bangle has to go on her arm first, before the others. The iron bangle is treated in exactly the same manner as the pair of conch-shell bangles, both being signs of a married woman. One will never find a married Hindu woman in Bengal whose husband is alive without her iron bangle. Even if the bangle is covered with silver or gold, it is still an iron bangle.

On the same day, the *ginnīmā* introduces the bride to the rest of the household. The *ginnī*—or any other elder woman of the house—takes the *kājal latā* and, writing the names of each relative on the floor, states the kinship status and relationship of each person to the bride. The woman writing on the floor asks the bride to read each name, after which the woman wipes it off and writes another. Except on this day, the bride is never to utter the names of those who come under "mother," "father," or elder sister categories of kin: HeB, HeBW and HFBS, HMZ/B and HMBS/D. With these persons the bride has to maintain a respect relationship. She is thus introduced to the hierarchy of women, some of whom live in the same place and share in the daily *saṇgsār* work. From the first day on, she is expected to act in accordance with the code of conduct of her new house in relation to all the people living there.

After the introductions the bride is shown around the house by her mother-in-law. She is shown the cooking area (*rānnā ghar*), where a large part of her time will be spent, and the *ṭhākur ghar*, where she is expected to share the worship of the *baṇgśa*'s *kuladebatās*. The deities have to be bathed and fed, and bride's *nanod*s cannot share in the *pūjā*s of their father's ancestral deity.

In the course of the first day the *śāsuṛī* will specify what she wants the bride to do in the *saṇgsār*'s daily work and how she expects her to behave toward the people in the house and the *kuṭum* of the house. The question of the *ghomṭā* (married women being often seen with the end part of their *sāri*s covering their heads) is decided by the *śāsuṛī*: should the bride use the *ghomṭā* when in the presence of the elder males of the house—including her own husband—or only when men unrelated to the house are around or when *kuṭum lok* arrive? Some *śāsuṛī* insist that their *boumā*s always cover their heads. A wife does not use the *ghomṭā* in her father's house, however, except when people from her husband's village appear. If a *śāsuṛī* orders her *boumā* to do *praṇām* to her son every time he leaves the house she must comply, even though he is her husband. This is an extreme case of respect, but if the *śāsuṛī* so demands, the *boumā*'s only recourse is to obey.

The welcoming rituals and the blessings having been completed, the women go about their work. At night, no ritual activities take place, this being *kāl rātri,* the inauspicious night. Guests from the neighborhood return home; others from out of town stay for the *bou bhāt* before departing for their own homes.

The *kanyā kañjali,* the ritual with which the bride servered her ties with her father's house, also establishes her new ties with her father-in-law's house (see Chapter 2). The transfer of gifts from her father to her father-in-law, the meaning of *iñdur māṭi,* and the role of women as wealth all mark the bride as a new person. The virgin is transformed by the ritual into a married daughter in her father's house and into a son's wife in her father-in-law's house. Residence, childbirth, and the carrying of a line are symbolized and expressed in this dual ritual.

There are significant parallels between the welcoming rites of the bride on the day the couple return to the groom's house and the farewell ritual extended to the groom by his mother as he embarks on the journey to the marriage. The *bidai* (farewell) of mother and son symbolizes a new status, marks a separation between mother and son. The son leaves to acquire a wife, to replace his mother with another woman, who will run his *saṇgsār* and bear his line. In the *bidai* ritual the mother washes her son's feet as she would for a child. She dries his feet with her *sāri*'s *ācal* while asking him: "My son, where are you going?" The groom answers: "I am going to bring you a lowly servant [*dāsī*] or a Lakṣmī, the deity of wealth." She asks three times, each time receiving the same answer. After the third reply the groom departs without looking back. He should not see his mother's face once he is gone from the house, and he should not come back even if he has left something important behind.[24]

This is the last time a mother washes her son's feet. He is no longer a child; he is now a complete person, capable of being the householder, of bearing new responsibilities. The washing of the feet signifies the severance of one kind of authority. Now the son is himself ready to fulfill his duty to the ancestors and to the house. Through marriage he can continue the male line established and maintained by *pitṛ puruṣ* (forefathers). The *adhikār* (right, responsibility) of the marriage is to maintain the line, and the duty of a son is to see that the line is carried on. Thus marriage serves as a passage for men as well. Washing the groom's feet symbolizes the *sissu*-mother relationship, one in which the child is under the mother's care and *adhikār*, so there is no *pāp* (sin) in the act, even though the groom would never normally allow anyone in a respect relation to him to touch his feet. The role is reversed in the marriage rite, the reversal signifying the end of one type of relationship. The son, like his father and forefathers, takes on a male role and follows in the path of the ancestors in the concern for the line. Like his father, the son brings a wife and begets sons. The bride replaces the role of the mother in this sense and, in turn, she repeats her own mother's role in the house. The marriage completes a girl and a boy; it foreshadows the coming of sons for the *baṇgśa*. Through sons, the groom becomes united to his forefathers and continues the vertical tie with them.

The Status of Married Women in Contrast to Virgins and Widows

The Virgin

The arrival of a girl's menstruation is a sure sign of her readiness for marriage. Since the performance of the menstrual rites makes the virgin's sexuality "operative," a *dagar meye* (a fully grown but unmarried girl) becomes a danger to men of her father's house. Marriage is the only way of removing the potential occurrence of impure acts: sexual intercourse with one's own men whether in marriage or outside marriage. Ideally, a woman is married to a nonblood and different-*gotra* male of the same caste. There are, however, women who never marry, who remain spinsters (*abibāhita meye*) in their father's house. Women whose husbands have died are *bidhobās* (widows) and continue to reside in their husband's mother's house. Even a cursory look at women in the life cycle reveals a contrast between married women (in an auspicious state), widows (in an inauspicious state), and virgins (neither auspicious nor inauspicious but in between the two categories).

A *kumāri* (virgin) can be either a young unmarried girl or an old spinster, but for the purposes of this analysis I mean the virgin past puberty who is ready to undertake the responsibilities of marriage. In the past, *kumāri* girls were given in marriage before the arrival of their menstrual flow since this is a girl's purest stage. At present only the low castes and Muslims insist on giving their girls in marriage before the first menstruation, though the young wife remains in her father's house until she achieves puberty. The majority of marriages are contracted long after puberty even though a girl becomes ready for marriage after her first menstrual flow. In such a situation, the menstrual rites are known as *natun biye*, "new marriage." For child-brides, the rites are called *anna biye*, "another marriage," and are performed in the virgin's father's house. The menstruation rites of the child-bride define her sexual maturity, and on the third day after the ritual the husband may take her to his house to consummate the marriage. The ritual accompanying the first menstrual flow is simple, yet clearly tied to the sexual aspects of marriage, to the union of male and female.

For the menstrual rites, the child-bride is seated alone in a room holding the *noṛā*, which resembles the *liṅga*, in her lap. She wears the *lajjā bastra* (marriage *sāri*) given by her husband and is seated in a darkened room (since evil spirits may attack a new bride). On this, the only occasion when the *śil* and *noṛā* are separated, the bride herself becomes the *yoni,* so that bride and *liṅga* together represent the perpetuation of the line. The *śil noṛā* also represent mother and child, with the child (*noṛā*) in turn standing for either the male seed or the husband through whom birth is accomplished (*bābā diye janma*). In this case the *noṛā* may stand for father or son, the one being encompassed by the other (the father in the son, and the son in the father's and the ancestors' lines).

The three days the virgin is kept in the room coincides with the three days of pollution accompanying each monthly menstrual flow. For those three days each month a woman cannot perform sacred works, must abstain from cooking, and may not touch the elders of the house. The pollution, however, affects the woman alone and is not extended to cover other male or female members of the household. For the three days of pollution the married woman does not use vermilion or *āltā,* nor does she oil or wash her hair. The rituals of birth and menstruation are intricately tied to the principles of marriage and procreation.[25] Menstrual rituals are also related to the Goddess of Children, Ṣaṣṭhī, who presides over marriage and birth for different reasons but in relation to the procreation of children and the giving of life.

A prepubescent girl is required for some rituals. In *kumāri pūjā* she represents female deities. In marriage rituals she is the *nitkanyā,* the opposite aspect of the bride; in a pure state, her sexuality does not pose a threat to the men of the house. The virgin who before puberty appears in rituals because of her purity (because she has not been touched by menstrual pollution) becomes impure to her own household after puberty. Following her menstrual flow the virgin is inauspicious for ritual purposes, though she becomes auspicious in relation to marriage. After marriage, menstrual impurity becomes positive, since a woman is united in marriage to a husband through whom she will bear children and continue the male line. Menstrual rites open one's sexuality and one's readiness to carry the male line.

The menstrual flow sets the *kumāri*'s dormant *matṛ śakti* in motion by making her capable of carrying the male seed and giving birth to a male child. Sharing the same blood and *gotra* renders the combination of seed and *matṛ śakti* impossible. This results in concern over the presence of unmarried women in the house, for it makes the presence bad and immoral. The virgin, by changing her status to *strī* in marriage, removes this fear of pollution, making her absence from the house good and auspicious. In her husband's house her status is that of a divinity, the bearer of legitimate children (*santān*), the living symbols of the male line.

Children born to an unmarried girl fathered by males of her father's house or other men "outside" marriage destroy the father's line. Children outside traditional Hindu marriage may also be those of intercaste marriages or of couples of the same caste who share blood or *gotra* before the marriage. All children from such unions are outcastes who belong to the mother and only to her in the eyes of the *samāj*. They carry no title, continue no line, for a woman cannot bear children for her father's line.

To break the line's code of conduct (*niyam karan*, rules for behavior) by bearing a child before marriage invariably harms the father's house since the *kumāri* is still in the father's care, in the same *baṇgśa* and *bhāiyat*, with the same *jñati* and *gotra*. Not only the father but all the *jñati* and *āttiya* are thus polluted. A child born after marriage, on the other hand, not only fulfills the aim of marriage but makes one's father's *kuṭum* into relatives by blood (*rakta āttiya*), binding two sets of lines closer together.

In general, the emphasis in a *kumāri*'s life with her father is on preparation for the duties and responsibilities of marriage. A *kumāri* is taught before marriage to model her life on that of her mother and the other married women of the house. She learns about kitchen lore, diseases and their cures, smaller ailments (pox and skin diseases) and the medication for them, and which deities to approach and how. She is instructed in the value of food items: what is eaten what time of the day, month, and season; for what purpose each vegetable or spice is consumed and what its effects are. Thus she is introduced to the knowledge and teaching of her father's *saṇgsār* but without responsibilities and without specific duties in relation to the house and its *kuladebatā*s. (The incoming women of the house [M, FBW, and BW] are the ones to care for the *kuladebatā*s.)

It is knowledge of the *śvaśur bāṛi saṇgsār* and its daily life that must take precedence over all other teachings. A young bride just about to settle in her husband's house is given specific guidelines for action and behavior in accordance with the *śvaśur bāṛi* code of conduct, which may be very different from that of her father's house. In preparation, she learns to be respectful to elders, to be ready to learn new sets of rules and behavior, and to become accustomed to the idea of leaving her own house for another. She learns to be docile and humble, to obey her in-laws' norms, and to sacrifice her likes and dislikes for the whole household's happiness and peace. Private happiness becomes secondary to that of the house as a whole. The incoming wife dissolves her individuality and becomes one of a collectivity.

The Wife

When a virgin becomes a wife (*bou, boumā*—wife, wife-mother) to her in-laws and to her husband (one's husband never being referred to as an in-law) she is canceled ("cut off") from her father's collection of ancestors in the line (*baṇgśa bali*). She is now of her husband's *gotra* and is added to his *baṇgśa bali*. The outgoing, married daughter is replaced by her brother's wife—her *boudī*—who becomes her children's *māmīmā* (MBW). The exchange of women, the giving and taking of daughters between houses and lines unrelated in terms of *gotra* and blood connection, removes the possibilities of incest, of a blood or classificatory union between brothers and sisters. Marriages between persons with similar *gotra*s are deemed incestuous since people with similar *gotra*s are considered brothers and sisters.

There are vast differences between married and unmarried women. Besides severing her ties with her father's house and adopting a new *gotra,* new ways of action, new residence, and a new set of relatives, a married woman must learn new rules for purity and pollution, new life cycle rites, new relationships, and new responsibilities. Some are similar to those of her father's house; others, drastically different.

Daily household duties are divided among all the women in the house, with the younger women's share being the greatest. Once the morning cooking is finished, there is more work to be done for the evening meals. The young bride will do whatever her mother-in-law tells her to do. She is expected to stay at home all the time unless accompanying elders of the house to the market, to the temple for worship at festival time, or to the local ashram to attend religious discourse. She is also expected to keep the elders company and to prepare *pān* for those who want it. She will ask her superiors' permission before going out of the house for visits to the neighborhood and to her father's house; she must obtain permission before doing anything not part of the daily household routine. Whether or not a new bride continues her college education depends on the wishes of her in-laws, irrespective of what her own father wants her to do. At times even her own husband cannot intervene on her behalf. Through marriage the bride acquires a new set of relations with whom she is united by a common bond, with whom her activities must cohere in a unified and consistent manner, with whom her actions should not clash.

The complete day of a married woman in her in-laws' house can be summarized briefly. The youngest wife of the house is the first to wake up in the morning. Changing the *sāri* she has slept in, she washes her face and hands and lights the permanent hearth (*onan*), a process which takes at least an hour. Tea is set up; milk is boiled for the children or the elderly. By the time the tea is ready, the rest of the people in the household begin to awake. She serves tea with biscuits and parched or puffed rice to both adults and children. If water is needed for a bath, the young wife helps draw water from the well. While everyone bathes and changes clothing, she puts away the beds and folds the bedding.

Those who work outside the house eat their cooked midday meal before leaving for work around 10 A.M. or so. This means that boiled rice, a lentil dish, a vegetable or two, and perhaps a small amount of fish or meat must be ready by the time the men and school children finish their baths. Having fed the children and men, the women wash the area where the food was served, clean the utensils, and sweep the cooking area. They may serve a light tiffin to those who have not yet had their rice meal. After taking their own baths there may be clothes to wash, though in some cases the larger pieces are sent to the Dhobā (washerman). After the remaining members of the house are fed, the young wife eats her rice meal. The dirty utensils are washed while the older members of the household rest for an hour or two. Tiffin is again served in the early afternoon. Children are dressed and girls have their hair combed, tasks that have to be done by the mothers, other married women, or elder sisters.

There are a few hours during the day when no specific work has to be done. The time between 4 and 6 P.M. is used to visit neighbors, temples, or an ashram. Younger girls and newly married women are accompanied by their mothers-in-law or other elder women of their houses. The outing is not a must for all women, but this is the time married women are relatively free from the *saṇgsār*'s work. Some women only go out once a week or once a month—others, daily—the frequency depending on their mothers-in-law's tolerance or intolerance. Many women stay at home and relax or attend to the very young or very old.

In the evening when the cows return home, the *saṇgsār*'s work begins again. Cows are fed and milked, children are helped with their lessons, and cooking is begun for the evening meal. Rice or *rutis* (wheat cakes) have to be prepared and vegetables must be cut and cooked. Once again the men and children are fed first, followed by the older women, and last the young married women. No *strī* will eat rice before her husband has finished his meal. Again, the feeding and cooking area is cleaned and the utensils washed and put away. Beds and bedding are laid out for everyone. Only after all the other people of the household have gone to sleep can the younger women retire.

The *kuladebatā* has to be worshipped daily either by one of the household's married women or a priest. On Tuesdays, Thursdays, and Saturdays, one does the weekly worship of various deities: Nārāyan, Lakṣmī, and Soni. The Thursday worship, that of Lakṣmī, is performed by most households in which there are married women. Though the worship is quite simple, preparation for it requires time and effort: the worship room must be cleaned and the deity washed, garlanded, and dressed before the ritual is actually performed.

Occasions such as birth, death, and marriage add to the work. In the case of birth, the mother herself is in a state of pollution and cannot participate in the work. Thus, more work is done by the other women, who not only take on the new mother's share of duties but also attend to her and the newborn baby, feeding them special food. Death in the house also means added household duties and restrictions in terms of cooking and worship.

One can see that it is the married women who run the *saṇgsār*. One can also see that most of the work is performed by the young married women. If a *boumā* is lazy, short-tempered, or sits idle all day, she is often rebuked by her mother-in-law and the older women. At times she is shamed in front of guests or close friends. The *śāsuṛī* cannot send a wife away to her father's house permanently, but she can make it impossible for her even to visit her father's house at festival times. But what about the older women, especially the mother-in-law? What transpires in the bazaar or in business is of little concern to her. Her world is the domain of the *saṇgsār*. As mistress of the house, she manages household activities and has command over responsibilities and events that relate to the *saṇgsār*. After ordering her sons' wives to perform specific duties, she retires to a world of worship and meditation.

The ideal is to have a harmonious relationship with one's mother-in-law, though this is seldom the case. I have mentioned the Bengali saying that one can never completely replace one's daughter with a *boumā*. *Śāsuṛī* and *boumā* are bound to face difficulties with each other and with the rest of the household, difficulties not easily overcome since the new bride cannot complain to her husband. Difficulties between a new bride and her mother-in-law are implied and demonstrated in some of the rituals. As wives in different generations of the same line, *boumā* and *śāsuṛī* are, in a way, fused in the same house. Therefore, to fight with one's mother-in-law would be to fight with one's mother—totally unacceptable behavior. To cope with this situation a girl depends on what she was taught in her father's house: to sublimate her troubles and unhappiness.

The incoming bride is introduced to the house as a deity personified, as the (line's) *baṇgśer* Lakṣmī, a phrase that carries a double meaning. First, it relates to notions of wealth, in goods and property as well as in a *santān* (son). Second, it refers to Lakṣmī's qualities of calmness, composure, beauty, and serenity. Like Lakṣmī, the bride is expected to be cool and at peace with all. In one of the rituals, she is asked to step on a pile of fresh cow dung (*gabar*)[26] placed in front of her. Cow dung, a sacred "thing of the cow" for both temple and house rituals, is noted for its coolness.

In addition to embodying the qualities and beauty of a deity, a newly married woman must embody the intelligence of an elder woman in *saṇgsār* activities. She has to know how to apportion and distribute the daily food among all the members of the house and how to delegate work to others. Married women are thus special persons in Bengali society—special in the worlds of both men and women—in being both deity and mother (*mā*). The ability to bear children is the sacred gift of all women, birth itself being a very auspicious ritual. The bride is likened to *Mā* Durgā, the ideal daughter-in-law who is patient and never complains. Durgā's annual visit to her father's house is likened to the journeys a married woman makes between her father's and her father-in-law's houses.

Married women in their in-laws' house spend a lot of time performing *brata*s and rituals dedicated to deities having to do with the house. *Brata*s are specifically women's rituals; they are vows or resolutions to worship a deity for a particular reason, the offering and the worship to be done before the boon is granted. Not all married women perform *brata*s but the majority still do. *Brata*s of the various deities not only define women in their roles as mothers, wives, and daughters but express ties of love, devotion, dependency, kinship, and related concerns of the house. At times, *brata*s and *strī ācār*s overlap, and at other times the two are distinct, although both are concerned with protection of relatives and maintenance of wealth and the health of husband and children. Some *brata*s and *pūjā*s require a fast of a half or a whole day. If a *bṛata* requires that at least one person fast, it is invariably the married woman, the mother, who does the fast.

The Widow

In the past, widows remained unmarried after the death of their husbands. Today, the government of India allows widow remarriage. Nonetheless, widow remarriage is either restricted to the world of novels and films or practiced in cities where the couple has no immediate kinship ties. It is rare for widows in villages or in rural towns to consider remarrying. The case is slightly different for lower castes, but even within this group the desire to be accepted as Hindus in the true sense forces them to follow the customs of the upper castes. *Sampradān,* the act of giving a virgin in marriage, is a single offer performed once in the lifetime of a girl; having been given once, she cannot be given again. After the death of her husband a woman remains a widow forever. Civil marriages or other types of marriage (such as those performed independently by a couple in front of a deity) are beyond any concern for *gotra,* blood, or even caste. Although a woman can remarry according to the civil law as long as her husband is dead before she contracts a second marriage, children born to a remarried widow belong to her alone; they are neither accepted as the children of her deceased husband's line nor given their father's title. A widow normally remains in her husband's house and follows the conduct applicable to a widow in her in-laws' house.

The remarriage of a widow within the household to relatives such as the husband's brother or other males of the house is out of the question. In the first place, both the widow and her husband's brother have the same *gotra.* More important is the fact that when the woman becomes a wife she becomes "half of her husband." A husband gives his new wife the symbols of a married woman: iron bangles and vermilion. Through his death, he takes away these symbols. Similarly, a woman offers her gifts of a *santān,* her reproductive organs, and her sexuality to her husband. When he dies these gifts are not returned, her reproductive power, her sexuality, and her femaleness being permanently removed. This means that the death of a man puts an end to the femaleness of his wife. After the death of the husband, a part of the woman is symbolically dead. The widow is neither a virgin who can be given to others in marriage nor a married woman with a living husband through whom children can be produced.

One might still ask why the *bidhobā* cannot remarry and carry the line of her husband. The case is more complicated than it initially appears. First, the house and line concerned would have to adopt a son (by changing his *gotra* with the help of the priest and the appropriate rituals). The newly adopted son would then be marrying his sister (same *gotra*), since the widow was also adopted at marriage into the same *gotra* and line. The marriage rules specifically state that persons of the same *gotra* before marriage cannot contract a marriage; thus such a marriage would not be concluded.

This is not the case for a widowed man. There is not even a term for a widowed man. A man can remarry in the sacred act of *biye* if his wife dies or if she proves barren (*banja*). A man acquires a woman in marriage and begets children through his wife, but he himself does not change in the process of marriage and does not take his wife's *gotra*. It is the woman that is united to the man in the marriage ritual, changing her *gotra* and adopting a new one. The case of a remarriage for a widowed woman is different from that for a man. Women change their *gotra* only once in a lifetime, at the time of marriage (or in adoption), whereas men only change *gotra* if adopted. Thus a man may repeat *sampradān* with another woman of the first wife's natal line or with a woman related to the line of the previous wife. If the first union was barren, a second wife may be brought in for the begetting of a child to carry the line.

The major fear of a married woman is becoming a widow. As a virgin, a girl does *brata*s to Śiva and Durgā, asking them for a husband like Śiva. After marriage, the same girl does a different set of rituals on a higher and more complex level to secure her husband's health and prosperity. Wives plead with the deities in *brata*s and *pūjā*s to keep their husbands and children alive; they fear becoming childless or widowed. Married women say that they never do worship for their own well-being since to be healthy yet to have a sick or dead husband would defeat the whole purpose of their existence. Once or twice a week married women are involved in the worship of one deity or another, all for the good of husbands and children.

Widowhood is a negation of marriage, of life with a husband. Death of one's *swāmī* destroys the union brought about by marriage: a union of male and female, the bringing together of male (*puruṣa*) and female (*śakti*) elements. Death separates the male and female complementarity (renewable by men but not by women), making the widow inauspicious in relation to *strī*s (married women) in the house. The widow is associated with death and a dead person, her dead husband. Barred from participating in many ritual aspects of the *saṇgsār*, she cannot worship the *kuladebatā* and can only cook for other widows in the household. Though both virgins and widows are inauspicious, the distinguishing factor is that virgins have the potential of becoming auspicious (marrying) while widows do not.

Widows go through a ritual in which they are deprived of their marriage symbols, a ritual *kumāri* girls and married women do not attend. The new *bidhobā* must move her iron bangle, break her conch-shell bangles, and throw both in the pond. Whatever else she has on her hands or neck must be removed, though these need not be thrown into water. Having removed her iron bangle and wiped the vermilion from her head, the widow takes a bath in the pond to complete her passage from the state of marriage to that of widowhood.[27]

The first set of widow's clothing is given to the widow by her own father or brother or any other male from her father's house. These consist of a petticoat worn with a white *sāri,* a *gumsi* (a red string tied around the waist), and a *bel mālā* (a necklace made of the sacred wood-apple), string and garland being worn at marriage and every life cycle ritual in which an individual passes from one stage to another. Her father or other males of her father's house help to lift her from the impurities caused by the death of her husband, impurities which pollute all members of the husband's male line.[28] People of her father's house assist the widow during the actual bathing. If there are no widows from her father's house, then other *bidhobā*s from the husband's house or from the neighborhood (*pāṛā*) come to help her as she enters the water a married woman for the last time and emerges a widow.

The widowhood bath, the *bidhobār snān,* is paralleled by the *biyer snān*s (marriage baths) and by the events narrated in the Manasā-Behulā myth where Behulā, the new bride, becomes a widow on her marriage day. With the bath on the day of marriage, the woman leaves behind her *eyo bora jiban* (youth, virginity). Like the young bride who leaves behind a completed stage of her life at the *śil noṛā,* the *bidhobā* does the same in a different way, starting an inactive life (*jiban*), leaving behind her married stage. At the time of marriage, a father offers his daughter her first married clothing (*bibāhita kapar*); so at the time of her husband's death the father or his son also gives the married daughter her first widow's clothing; no *āltā* or pair of shell bangles are given. The bathing of the bride and the widow become an inversion of each other; one ends and the other begins a union of female and male.

A widow remains in her husband's house and shares in some work of the *saṇgsār,* but she has to conform to the widow's code for conduct of her in-laws. Though widows are in an inauspicious state, one must note that their inauspiciousness differs from house to house and that widows—especially the elder ones—are respected in Bengali society. A widow is knowledgeable in regard to the *saṇg-*

sār. A widowed mistress of the house remains the woman in charge. In most cases her power in the house actually increases. It is up to her either to continue running the household herself or to give the full control to her children. A widowed mother can give a daughter in marriage; she can do the *sampradān*. Her touch is not inauspicious to the bride or the groom since a widowed mother's touch is not inauspicious to her own children; the death, having occurred within the house, affects only the members of that line and house. The widow, on the other hand, will not touch an outside bride. At marriages many of the invited widows assist in some of the work. They may prepare betel chew and *pān*, cut vegetables, grind spices, and clean fish, although they may neither cook and serve food nor help the bride or groom dress. Widows will not participate with married women in the *strī ācār*s, and after *gāe halud* they may not touch the couple, who are then in a pure state.

After the death of her husband, a widow says that her *hāṛi* (cooking clay pot) is "removed," "set aside," "lifted up," meaning that she does not cook for the *saṇgsār*, does not cook for a husband. Instead, she now shares another's cooking pot; she remains a member of the house and is fed, clothed, and sheltered. There are a few restrictions a widow must follow, and such rules she learns from other widows in the neighborhood. Her diet is strictly vegetarian, and her consumption of rice is limited to one time a day. In place of cooked rice at other meals she may eat dried or parched rice (*cira* or *muṛi*) or *ruti*s (flat bread) made out of wheat. She has to wear a white *sāri* without any border because a red border signifies the married status.

Young widows confine themselves to the house, but old widows do not. There are groups of elderly widows who meet every afternoon to sit and gossip about other widows or married women. Sometimes they congregate to recite the Mahābhārata or the Rāmāyana or simply praise the name of Lord Kṛṣṇa. To some extent, there is a trend among widows to modernize widowhood. In the past, widows cropped their hair and wore borderless white *sāri*s. Today, special off-white *sāri*s with narrow, light colored borders are appearing on the market. Some widows wear these *sāri*s and keep their hair long. Widows are even seen wearing gold and silver bangles. But even with these innovations in widowhood, a widow still does not wear an iron bangle, conch-shell bangles, or vermilion, for an iron bangle and vermilion can only be worn by married women and conch-shell bangles are a father's gift to a virgin.

The widow stands in a position parallel to a *kumāri*: both can cause potential ruin to a male line by using their sexuality and bearing children in an unmarried state. The difference between the two women is evident and culturally defined: a widow is the antithesis of the *kumāri,* who is auspicious, pure, and untouched by death. Widows await completion in their own deaths; *kumāri*s await completion in marriage.

CHAPTER 4

Marriage and the Statuses of Women

The Meaning of Marriage in India

The Institution of Marriage in Indian Society

For Hindus, marriage is a sacred union, indissoluble, irrevocable, a union for a lifetime; it is the most auspicious *samṣkār*. The sacred conception of marriage in India can be traced back to the age of the Vedas. The Satapatha Brāhmaṇa declares that a man is complete only when in union with a woman through marriage.[1] Manu states that "without house, without home, without progeny [a wife] makes him; he becomes without succession, he is destroyed."[2] According to Manu, procreation is a male's duty. Procreation is the purpose of marriage so immortality can be achieved. A son is represented in Hindu art and writing as one who can offer prayers, worship, and honor to the gods. The threefold duties a Brāhmaṇ son must fulfill are pupilage to the *ṛṣi* (seers), sacrifice to the gods, and offerings to the *pitṛ*s (ancestors) (Kapadia, 1947: 90). The last duty is shared by all castes, but only Brāhmaṇs can perform sacrifice for the gods and recite the *mantra*s for the sacrifice.[3]

Manu regards marriage as an individual and social necessity. He calls it "*śarīra samaṣkāra* (sacrament of life and body) through which every man and woman muṣt pass at the proper age and time" (see Das, 1962: 113). He says the aims of Hindu marriage are *dharma* (duty), *praja* (progeny), and *rati* (pleasure). *Dharma*, sacred duty, dominated Manu's idea of marriage; progeny was the secondary result (being of course related to *dharma*); and pleasure was relegated to the last place in his hierarchy. Marriage was and is "considered to be sacred because it is said to be complete only on the performance of the sacred rites accompanied by the sacred formulae" (Kapadia, 1958: 168).

A discussion of Hindu marriage is necessarily inadequate if it overlooks the caste system, kinship, and the sacred domain.[4] The implication of the caste system for marriage (and vice versa) as viewed through the ideology of *karma* (fate), *dharma* (duty), and *punar janma* (reincarnation) is essential to a study of marriage. Marriage rules and regulations, the position of brides and mothers, and the giving and taking are practices established in the classical Hindu writings. Here I agree with Khare (1972) that caste cannot be seen independently of kinship and marriage and that the latter form a part of a wider whole wherein caste order need not be the central concern (see also Van der Veen, 1972: 32). Although caste prohibition has loosened (some caste rules such as those governing intercaste dining are no longer rigidly observed), caste endogamy still prevails in marriage. Intercaste marriage, allowed and even encouraged by the government of India, is still rare.

Marriage and the Caste System

Hindus believe that their social system is divinely ordained, controlled, and oriented (Mathur, 1964). This view is an indigenous conceptualization of the integrative role of religion in society, the social order being expressed and reaffirmed by the ideology and vice versa. The ideology itself helps to integrate and perpetuate that social order through the notions of *dharma* (duty), *artha* (self-interest), and *karma* (destiny). It enters into the ordering of caste relations through myths, ritual prescriptions and prohibitions, ceremonies and festivals, revealing the larger system in the relations among its constituent and interdependent parts.

A hierarchical system of castes is the basis of the social structure. Caste status is acquired by birth and all castes are endogamous hereditary groups. In ideal terms, castes also represent traditional occupations, thus expressing a horizontal division of Indian society according to labor. The main features of the caste system are generally taken to be segmental division of society; hierarchy; restrictions on food and drink in social intercourse; civil and religious disabilities and privileges accorded to different castes; restricted choices in occupation; and restrictions on marriage (Kannan, 1963). This study pertains both to the way the caste system organizes, restricts, influences, and expresses marriage and to the ways marriage determines and symbolizes the caste system.

From the starting point of Bougle's definition of the caste system, Dumont analyzes caste society as "divided into a larger number of permanent groups which are at once specialized, hierarchized and separated (in matters of marriage, food and physical contact) in relation to each other" (Dumont, 1961: 34). These three principles rest on a fundamental conception and principle, the opposition of pure and impure. By hierarchy Dumont means a ladder of command, the lower rungs of which are encompassed by the higher ones in a regular succession. This gradation involves neither power nor authority but only the "principle by which the elements of a whole are ranked in relation to the whole" (Dumont, 1970a: 66), with Hindu religion providing a view of that whole. Dumont is concerned with economic and political power to the extent that these articulate with the overriding emphasis on hierarchy, purity, and pollution in India. The fundamental structural principle is the polarity of pure and impure.

> Castes are arranged in a hierarchical order according to the relative degree of purity that can be attributed to each in their relations to each other, as well as to the whole, i.e., the Brahman, whose purity "encompasses" the whole caste system. The opposition of pure and impure is contradictory in itself and mutually exclusive, hence the possibility of building a relational model on these principles (Pocock, 1957: 24).

Thus to grasp the sociological significance and the meaning of the religious concepts of ritual purity and impurity, one must also comprehend the separation of power and status in Indian cultural terms. Dumont notes that the divergence of economic and political power and religious status (a separation with which he deals neither extensively nor adequately) can be discovered in the more specific contexts of marriage, economic exchange, and the sacred gift. My Chapters 1 and 2 discuss the problems of separating status and power in relation to *sampradān* and *pon* clarify the two domains as distinguishable yet closely related, with power and status complementary to each other.

In marriage, caste principles and rules regulate and dictate one's choices. As noted by Tambiah, "despite the growth of modifications over time and dialectal regional variations over space, the main architectural principles of the Indian edifice of family and marriage appear to have remained remarkably intact" (Tambiah, 1973a: 74). Intercaste marriages (referred to as "love marriages") fall outside the realm and principles of Hindu society, which neither accommodates nor tolerates them. Although intercaste marriages take place, they have not succeeded in changing the Hindu marriage system. Such changes in behavior have little or no effect on caste ideology; as a result, the caste structure has not been fundamentally affected by modernization or westernization (Srinivas, 1966b).[5] *Jāti* endogamy amounts to an obligation to marry within one's segmental caste group. This is one of the fundamental principles directly related to women and marriage.

In his work on the Patidars in the Gujarat region of west India, Pocock suggests that it is through marriage within the caste that a Patidar recognizes and is recognized by caste fellows: "In this regard marriage affirms the equality of the contracting parties" (Pocock, 1972: 94). The Patidars have rules allowing hypergamous marriages for the process of inclusion and exclusion of specific parties, although this flexibility is not shared by all castes. "Unity of the *jāti* is based on the acceptance of marriage relationships. By refusing to marry daughters to lower groups, but by accepting brides from them, the higher group manages to settle the incompatibility of inclusion and exclusion" (Pocock, 1957: 13).

Hypergamy is marriage to someone of a higher social status.[6] It is very important that one thinks in terms of the man or of the woman in using this terminology, otherwise each marriage would be both hypergamous and hypogamous. In both hypergamous and hypogamous marriages the statuses are differentiated, the important point being what is passed on to the legal descendants of a marriage (Van der Veen, 1972: 98). In Bengal, descent is traced in the male line. The children of a woman belonging to a higher or lower status line than her husband receive the same social status as the father. With the exception in the past of Rāhṛī-Brāhmaṇ and Kāyastha Kulinism, classical hypergamy—the prohibition of women marrying into an inferior group—is not a crucial issue in Bengali marriages.[7]

Despite the absence of formal hypergamy in Bengali marriages, hierarchical elements enter the marriage sacrament. The superiority of the bride-receivers and the inferior position of the bride-givers entails a ritual, though not a terminological differentiation of wife-givers and wife-takers. The inferior/superior relationship is limited to the giving and receiving of the gift of a virgin. Kinship terminology of consanguines and affines does not mark a superior/inferior distinction between givers and receivers. On the contrary, the two sets of fathers-in-law and mothers-in-law are in a completely reciprocal relationship to each other (Fruzzetti and Östör, 1976b). Wife-givers are obligated to keep giving in the form of gifts and prestations, but since a reversal of marriages is acceptable, the relationship of giving and taking may also be reversed (a seeming paradox which I discussed in Chapter 1).

Dowries are prevalent and serve as a foundation to any caste-Hindu marriage. Bride-givers offer a dowry in addition to the gift of the virgin.[8] Exchange marriages are encouraged, and this reversal in the direction of marriage works contrary to the notion of hypergamy, where women—as goods—are supposed to flow in only one direction. "The subordinate role of the bride givers finds expression first and foremost in the rule that the father of the girl should take the initiative in arranging a marriage [for his daughter]"; he has to approach the groom's side with the offer of his daughter (Van der Veen, 1972: 56). The absence of hypergamy in marriage does not account, however, for the unidirectional flow of gifts and prestations to the bride-receivers. The status of women and the meaning of marriage in terms of the individual in Bengali society help clarify the hypergamous characteristics that do enter into Bengali marriages.

Bengali Kinship and Marriage

Unlike in south India, where the terminological system clearly spells out the distinction between consanguines and affines and demarcates the marriageable categories from the unmarriageable, in Bengal, marriage rules and regulations do not. Yalman argues that in south India "the main function of the Dravidian kinship categories is to integrate marriage and sexual relations inside bilateral and largely endogamous kindreds" (Yalman, 1962: 548; see also Tambiah's 1965 critique). In a different context, Dumont also finds a system and a structure to south Indian kinship terminology, "since in marriage alliance the terminology fully accords with affinal relationships. In this sense terms taken to be 'kin-terms' yield a universe, systemic and similarly structured throughout the different levels and express parsimonious relationships between wife-givers and wife-takers" (Fruzzetti and Östör [on Dumont], 1976b: 65; see also Dumont, 1953 and 1957). These relationships are based on the parity between brothers-in-law that results in the maintenance of the marriage exchanges through succeeding generations within the terminological rules for marriage. In north India, however, the terminological system does not yield an unambiguous distinction between wife-givers and wife-takers and does not point to clear marriage rules.

Vatuk (1969) argues that there are indications of a marriage rule in the north India Hindu kinship terminology, but she does not formulate it clearly. Furthermore, she argues that hypergamy, unidirectional marriage, and separate local descent groups and kindreds have to be invoked outside the terminology as such to make sense of the marriage system. Fruzzetti and Östör's study of Bengali kinship terminology concludes that terminology is not a guide for marriage (in terms of who is a consanguine and who is an affine, who is marriageable and who is not) and that the terminology does not lead to any groups, whether or not these be in wife-giving, wife-taking, shared-descent, lineal, or genealogical blood relationships to each other. In that study, we state that "since only ego based groups are involved in marriage relationships (the spectacular clusters of kin-terms all being ego based) we are to account for an almost indefinitely extensible universe" (Fruzzetti and Östör, 1976b: 44). We found no concrete, ranked groupings of kin and affines in the terminological system. The Bengali terminological system did not elicit marriage rules.

Where then should one look for the expression of marriage rules? In caste relations? It is my contention that caste, kinship, and marriage relations can be elucidated only by a consideration of the Bengali concept of the person, which is, in turn, impossible to comprehend without the study of the women's domain of action, marriage rituals, conception, and birth. In the next few pages I will relate the concept of the person within the domain of women's action. Through marriage and birth rituals we will arrive at the meaning of kinship.

Daughters are given to the members of one's own caste group (*jāti,* caste, or subcaste cluster in a locality). But they cannot be given to those of the same *rakta* and *gotra. Rakta* is, however, not a gloss for genealogy since the kinship terminology does not give rules for the construction of "relatives," does not demarcate relatives from nonrelatives, and does not give rules for who can and who cannot be married among those already related. The widest and most definite group of one's relatives are those in one's *sapiṇḍa* and one's *bhāiyat.*

The *sapiṇḍa* are those with whom one shares blood through, as I have said, a common ancestor going back seven generations on one's father's side. Persons thus related offer *piṇḍa,* a sacrifice, to the same group of ancestors. Ancestors on one's father's side are *gotraja sapiṇḍa* (*sapiṇḍa* of the same *gotra*), and those on one's mother's side are without *gotra sapiṇḍa* (*bhinna gotra*). Smriti laws prohibit marriage within the *sapiṇḍa.*[9] A *sapiṇḍa* relationship entails sharing parts of the same body directly or indirectly through the indigenous construction of blood. Males of a *baṅgśa* invariably belong to the same *sapiṇḍa*. Although women pass from their own (father's) *gotra* to that of their husband when they marry, they retain a link to their father's *sapiṇḍa* through blood. Blood is transmitted in the male line, so this link between a married woman and her father ends with her death.

The importance of women in determining *rakta, gotra,* and *sapiṇḍa* as well as marriage relations (and the impact of them on society at large) is shown by Van der Veen's study of marriage. In discussing the Anavil Brāhmaṇs, he states that his data are incomplete because, having worked with men, his information about *gotra, rakta,* and *sapiṇḍa* is insufficient. Hence, certain problems come up in his conclusions: "Both the father and mother contribute particles of their own body to the birth of a child, *sapiṇḍa* here means cognates from father's as well as mother's side" (Van der Veen, 1972: 86). For the Anavil Brāhmaṇs, the rules forbid a man to marry a woman who is his agnate in the line of ascent through the father as far back as the fifth generation. But what of the mother's male ancestral line? Why then is there no marriage allowed with the mother's side when a married woman becomes a part of her husband's *sapiṇḍa*?

One's *sapiṇḍa* relatives are those who give a mixture of cooked rice and other items as an offering to the same ancestors in the *śrāddha* (death rituals). One's *sapiṇḍa* ancestors are the *sātpuruṣ*, the seven generations of one's ancestors in the male line: "But while *sātpuruṣ* refers to male relatives in male-linked layers above oneself . . . branching out from the apex of a triangle to a broad base around oneself . . . the *sapiṇḍa* refers to the same triangle through the offering of food to ancestors in mortuary rituals" (Fruzzetti and Östör, 1976a: 81–82). Both cases specifically refer to the seven generations of fathers. Therefore *piṇḍa* is offered to the *sātpuruṣ* because one shares their blood.

Birth and death pollution clearly identify one's *sapiṇḍa* relatives since the pollution affects all those linked in the male line. As Tambiah points out, "Death and birth pollution essentially refer to the bodily and therefore kinship connection between status equals. Death and birth pollute kinsmen by virtue of this connection alone" (Tambiah, 1973b: 210). Thus death pollution (*mṛittaśauc*) distinguishes those linked through *sapiṇḍa* (and, to a lesser degree, *gotra* ties) from those linked by marriage alone, for the pollution affects only one's blood and *gotra* relatives in the *sapiṇḍa* and *bhāiyat* groups.

Living *sapiṇḍa* relatives also fall within the *bhāiyat,* the group of persons with whom one shares blood in a recognizable form through birth, male to male. But this unit is counted only up to the *sātpuruṣ* degree, this being also the group which must observe the pollution and purificatory rites. Pocock discusses the role of the *bhāiyat* in terms of "the etiquette of invitations and rights of hospitality." One can assume, he says, that food and hospitality are extended to this group at any time: "The sociological relevance of *bhāiyat* to the development of larger groups is implicit in the etiquette of invitations and the rights of hospitality I have referred to. The etiquette expresses the balance between the desire for the relationship and the fear of being too much obliged" (Pocock, 1972: 87). But Pocock does not clearly distinguish the other factors which separate the *bhāiyat* from other groups of relatives; he fails to relate the concepts of purity and pollution to the *bhāiyat*. The death of a *bhāiyat* relative obligates the living members of that person's *bhāiyat* to observe the line's prescribed period of pollution. This period of pollution is ascribed to each caste group in accordance with their system of belief and ritual as set out in the sacred texts.

Shah offers an additional explanation of the ties between these groups. He claims that patrilineal descent groups are bound together by the giving of funeral oblations to their ancestors and that the unit that is invited to offer oblations to the dead is not necessarily the same as the household unit. Nevertheless, he states that the ritual unit corresponds to and coincides with the *bhāiyat* unit:

> Not only was the ritual unit the same as the property unit, many writers of classical texts discussed the property question in relation to the question of who should perform the *shraddha* for whom. They argued that a man inherited property from an ancestor because he propitiated him. The legal definition of the joint family therefore tended to coincide with and be sanctioned by the definition of the circle of persons required to perform the *shraddha* (Shah, 1974: 25).

Joint property is held by the male members of a line and is inherited by males of the *bhāiyat*.[10]

Funerary rites are related to the concepts of relatives and groups of relatives, such as the *bhāiyat*. *Sapiṇḍa* relatives are affected by each others' death pollution, and each *sapiṇḍa* relative must observe the rituals of pollution and its removal. The three major funerary rites the *bhāiyat* must follow are: first, offering libations of water to the dead at the cremation; second, observing a 10- to 30-day state of impurity; third, performing a major ritual in honor of the dead on the last day of mourning. A married daughter, although she has changed her *gotra* through marriage, retains blood ties with her father.[11] That this is so is shown by the traditional offering of libations to a deceased married daughter. To a Hindu, the great significance of marriage is, as I have said, that it is entered into for the procreation of a son. For the son will perform the *śrāddha* rituals of his father and the ancestors. The funeral rites performed together in effect continue the line and its obligations, all sharing in the repayment of a debt to the ancestors of the group (Kapadia, 1947: 209).

Of the persons who share blood, some "fall within the *bhāiyat*" (*bhāiyat moddhe pore*) and some remain outside. *Bhāiyat*s share the same male blood, maintained and carried through male lines. This fact differentiates the *bhāiyat* from *kuṭum* (marriage relatives and relatives from the maternal side—MB, *māmā*'s side). It is in this distinction that the Bengali nature of the construct "blood" is most clearly revealed. The distinguishing factor for the *bhāiyat* is blood itself. *Rakta,* then, is the substance people share in a brother relationship through the succession of males as brothers, fathers, and father's brothers. Blood is the significant discriminator among relatives both for inclusion among the *bhāiyat* and for exclusion for marriage in the formation of alliances. Women from one's *bhāiyat* (because they share blood) are given to non-*bhāiyat* men as wives. Since married women still retain blood ties with their father's *bhāiyat,* their children cannot in turn be taken as wives or husbands by their maternal relations.

Persons who are synchronically related to one another through seven generations are one's *sātpuruṣ, sapiṇḍa,* and *bhāiyat,* so these terms, therefore,

> refer to the same group of relatives . . . linked together in the same manner. The differences among these categories are recognized in terms of more or less extension along the same line, persons nearer or farther away from oneself, mainly living or mainly dead relatives within the same group (Fruzzetti and Östör, 1976a: 83).

Persons who individually (not in groups) belong to these units are known as *jñati,* but a *jñati* is also any person to whom one is related through the male line. Hence *jñati* ties can extend beyond the *sātpuruṣ* and *sapiṇḍa* groups (with their generational limitation). Yet within the *bhāiyat, jñati* refers to a person, not to a group: "Blood is traceable by implication since persons in the *bhāiyat* share the father's blood. But just as blood defines brotherhood, so male-linkedness defines the *jñati*" (Fruzzetti and Östör, 1976a: 84). *Jñati* may also observe each others' death and birth pollution, but the relationships may be so distant that the observation of the purificatory rites is not obligatory.

It is clear from this account of links among relatives—which is conceived in Bengali terms—that traditional kinship studies do not help one to understand the Bengali case. Kinship terms neither yield marriage rules nor point unambiguously to the boundaries of different kin groupings. Yet, as I have shown, there are groups of relatives in Bengal that can be discussed in terms of the indigenous construction of blood and marriage. There are *jñati* and *kuṭum* relatives; groups such as *bhāiyat, sapiṇḍa,* and *sātpuruṣ*; and *baṇgśa*s and *gotra*s. In all of these, blood, male line, pollution, and marriage seem to play central and determining roles. However, the seemingly clear picture of a patrilineal, segmentary lineage society is confused by the membership of women in these groups. Women change some of their kinship relationships to persons and groups on their marriage while retaining others. This in-a-line and of-a-line, blood continuity and *gotra* change, blood transmission and blood retention of women seems paradoxical yet is crucial for an understanding of kinship and marriage (the notion of *gotra, sapiṇḍa,* blood, and marriage relationships) and, through these, of caste society.

There are no universal, functional, or typological rules for analytically separating and then relating caste, kinship, and marriage. Caste and kinship groups are indistinguishable once indigenous categories are fully considered. Marriage is again the key to the system: it is through marriage endogamy and exogamy that these groups (*jñati, bhāiyat, gotra,* and *sapiṇḍa*) articulate, and the significance of that ceremony can only be appreciated through an examination of what women transmit and how, what constitutes the person, and what is blood continuity and ritual change in marriage.

Life Cycle Rituals and Their Significance in Bengal

One of the most effective ways to study women is through analysis of life cycle rituals. These rites (including *brata*s, *strī ācār*s, and other forms of ritual action and worship) focus on women, either by marking the transition from one status to another or by establishing relations among various categories of women in relation to other aspects of society. Marriage is a clear case where a female passes from one status (*kumāri,* prepuberty virginity) to another—that of a married woman (*bibāhita meye*). A married woman severs ties with her father's household to start life anew in her husband's house. The rites surrounding birth (which gives the most important culturally defined role to a Bengali woman) delineate the mother's new role in contrast to that of the new bride. The series of purificatory rites indicate her new status and her reintegration into the women's world as well as into the wider society. Yet, life cycle rituals, like marriage or kinship, cannot be studied as ends in themselves. As a kind of religion, they have to be studied in the context of women's activities, as an open-ended process in the formation and interpretation of the women's world.

Life cycle rites clearly define female sex roles within the totality of Bengali culture. I am not, however, advocating the separation of a private and a public domain with women participating in the former and men in the latter. In Bengal there is an indigenous opposition between household, everyday life and market, politics, and so forth; but these oppositions are not mutually exclusive, and a complete study of one does not discard the possibility of complementarity between male and female domains in action.

Women's rituals at marriage complement and at times form a part of the rituals performed by the Brāhmaṇ priest or other male participants of the same household. The male/female complementary aspect can also be found in the myths and rituals of everyday life. Life cycle rites (*saṃskāra*s, purificatory and sacramental rites) also demarcate the women's ritual domain. The creation and development of a person through the different stages applicable to male and female constructs is expressed and defined in these rituals, particularly through the marriage *strī ācār*s when analyzed in indigenous terms.

The institution of marriage combines the participation of male and female persons in a social group. Women and Brāhmaṇ priests are both ritualists, the marriage ceremonies emphasizing the unity of the two spheres of action, *strī ācār*s and Brahmanic rites, private and public, and *puruṣa* and *prakriti*. Through ritual, women maintain a distinctive role in Bengali society. Women are separate but they are not excluded from the public sphere; rather, the relations among domains are differently constructed.[12] Women's rituals express the separateness as well as the relatedness between male- and female-dominated spheres of activity. Rituals are the best place for looking at the indigenous definition of a woman's world and within that world at the complementarity of male and female as it affects *all* domains of Bengali society.

As previously stated, marriage is an obligation toward the ancestors and the community. There are certain rites which must be performed for the marriage to be complete, the main rites being *homa* (or fire sacrifice), *pāṇi grahaṇa* (taking the hand of the bride), and *saptapadi* (the bride and bridegroom taking seven steps together). These rites are performed by the Brāhmaṇ priest accompanied by the recitation of *mantra*s. Hindu marriage is a sacrament because it is said to be complete only on the performance of the sacred rites and the incantation of sacred formulas.[13]

Women's ritual activities in day-to-day life do not simply end with the performance of life cycle rites but revolve around *brata*s and *strī ācār*s, as well as rituals performed for the household and other deities. These performances are integrated into rituals and tied to the *pūjā*s of the annual calendar. Here I want to emphasize again that women's actions being separate does not necessarily imply that they are cut off from the rest of society. The rites of women are tied to *pūjā*s, life cycle rites, belief, kinship and other social relations, and the cultural system of the Bengali people as a whole; men and women are in complementarity, as this is defined in indigenous terms.[14]

What Happens to Women in Marriage

Male and female (*puruṣa* and *prakriti*) create lines (*baṇgśa*); they originate an issue (*santān*) in and through marriage. Marriage continues lines and brings together lines created by past marriages. Marriages also establish links among present lines. The originator of the line shares a blood relationship with subsequent segmentary lines; a relation endures through time and space via male descent and marriages. Marriage is entered into for the sake of the ancestors; otherwise the male line would end just as a married woman's father's line ends with her, since only sons can pass on the line. The exchange of women between and among lines maintains, continues, and links lines to each other.

According to marriage rules one's own women cannot become the vehicles through which men transmit their blood and lines; a sister cannot give life to a blood brother's seed (*bīj*). One's male blood relatives are brothers and fathers to the women of the line. Women outside the direct male line and the mother's father's line can become mothers of a man's children, and only in this capacity can women maintain ties with the ancestors (of their husbands).

Wives are the vehicles, receptacles through which men ensure the immortality of their line. Carter (1973) argues that at marriage women become blood relatives to their husbands. He also states that only by marrying a woman of suitable status can a man transmit unaltered to his children the status received from his father. I question, however, the passage of an "unaltered status" from father to son through a mother who has become a blood relative of her husband in the marriage ritual. Carter's ethnocomponential approach does not make clear why women become "of" the husband's blood at marriage. I also question the accounts of David (1974) and of Inden and Nicholas (1977). Carter, writing about and supporting Inden and Nicholas's work on kinship, states that in "North India as in South India, concepts of kinship are segmentary and marriage is thought to alter a woman's blood and kinship status" (Carter, 1973: 32). I agree that there is a change of kinship status; I argue throughout this study that women do not undergo a change of blood through marriage.

In Bengali marriage women undergo a change of status through a change of *gotra*. Through the ritual a woman leaves her father's line and is adopted into the *baṇgśa* of her husband and husband's father. The incoming wife of a male line is not seen, however, as undergoing a bodily transubstantiation at marriage; she neither changes to nor adopts her husbands' blood (*rakta*). Married women continue to share their father's and brother's blood. Only their *gotra* ties with their father's side change at marriage.[15]

Marriage (*biye*)—the giving of a daughter (*sampradān*) and the making of a groom into a close relative (a son-in-law, or *jāmāi*)—establishes a relationship between two previously unrelated households and lines. Relationships established through marriage (classed as *kuṭum-āttiya*) in one generation become blood relationships in the next; the "givers" of a woman become related to the "receivers" of that woman. The ritual process of making a daughter into a son links several sets and categories of relatives to each other. Two fathers-in-law (*śvaśur*) are *kuṭums* to each other and blood relatives to their son's and daughter's children.

In Bengal (and, with some exceptions, in the rest of India) blood is passed in the male line and descent is recognized through males, from fathers to sons. But blood is not merely biological; it is also a cultural contract. Blood refers to a substance that is enduring and persistent, a permanent attribute which is recognized, passed, and transmitted through the male members of a line with wives acting as carriers.

Women are brought into a line so that the men of the *baṇgśa* can continue their lines; they act as the carriers of the progeny, through the male blood. A new wife continues, however, to be a blood relative of her father (*bābā*) mother (*mā*), brother and sister (*bhāi* and *bon*), a mother's brother (*māmā*), a mother's sister (*māsī*), a father's brother (*kākā*), and all those people she considered blood relatives before her marriage. It is the maximal line of her father in which she is no longer a member. Her *gotra* is now the one into which she is married. Apart from the *gotra* of her husband, a married woman has none. At marriage a woman also ends her membership in her father's *sapiṇḍa* (cf. Shah, 1974: 114).

Marriage is entered into so that a man can fulfill his duty (*dharma*) of continuing the line, pleasing the ancestors, and—finally—reaping the joys of marriage. Each marriage establishes a line, a segment of a whole which is looked at in terms of the past male lines extending through three, five, or seven generations. The newborn child is related to the originator of the line through descent. A wife makes the immortality and longevity of the male line possible by transmitting and giving "life to the seed" of her husband (or the male blood); she does not transmit the blood of her father. Yet women, as mothers, do contribute blood to the child in the womb. The contribution is itself culturally constructed as augmenting the male seed (*bīj*), the blood of the male line. Women conceive of themselves as the field (*khettra*) and men as the cultivators of the field and as the seed sown into the field.[16]

Women receive the male blood (blood creates semen, semen creates blood) and give it life, power, and motion, nourishing and augmenting it with their blood. Women further nourish and augment the growth of the child through breast milk. Birth (*janma*) is given by the mother and recognized by the father (contrasting the giving, *janmadātā,* to the recognition, *paricay*). Birth is culturally constructed as being made possible through the father (*bābā diye janma,* or *pitṛ janma*), given and nurtured by the mother (*janmadātā mā*). As one can see, the mother complements her husband in the conception of a child. Nonetheless, the Bengali notion of blood, which carries the male line, is the father's seed. Blood in this context symbolizes maleness, in relation to the line which will be continued through male blood.

The Relevance of Ritual to the Social Relations of Women

Hindu marriage is a sacrament (*saṃskāra*) and as such requires sacred rituals that, though intertwined, can be separated into two forms: Brahmanic rituals handed down from Vedic times and *strī ācār*s performed locally by married women without a Brāhmaṇ priest and without Sanskrit *mantra*s. Both types of ritual are concerned with the same theme: male and female union through the complementary roles of the sexes in securing the immortality of the male line.

Vedic and Śāstric rituals are performed by Brāhmaṇ priests. With the use of sacred incantations (*mantras*) and formal rites, a priest enacts the role of the gods in the marriage ceremony. Vedic and Śāstric rites begin with purifications of the body and of the area where the rituals are performed, and they build up to the invocation and appearance of the gods as witnesses to the joining of a man and woman in sacred union.

Through *strī ācār*s, married women attempt to achieve the same results as do the priests in the more complex Brahmanic ritual forms (*pūjā*s). The types of *strī ācār*s are varied and numerous, every life cycle being filled with different rites.[17] The time Bengali women spend in their performance and their acute concern for proper observance of the rites indicate the importance of *strī ācār*s to them. The relationships of the rites to each other, to the larger domain of *pūjā*s and to the concepts of purity and pollution become evident when the women's activities are analyzed.

Through the married women's rituals, women: (1) enact the day-to-day (*saṇgsār*) concerns of the household; (2) portray the roles of wives, mothers, mothers-in-law; and (3) express their fears of becoming widows or remaining barren, and their hopes of acquiring wealth. These concerns are of course interrelated in everyday life. The rituals are further intended to sanctify marriage and to propitiate the gods and spirits of dead ancestors. Through the rituals women attempt to avert the influence of the "evil spirit" (*khārāp biddha*).

*Brata*s (a form of women's rituals devoted to different deities), which parallel *strī ācār*s, are rituals married women perform for the auspiciousness and good (*maṅgal*) they desire for their relatives. A *brata,* as compared to a *strī ācār,* is more in the order of a contract between the worshipper and the deity, being a vow or resolution to perform a sacred act provided the deity in question fulfills the worshipper's desire and request.

In women's rituals—both *strī ācār*s and *brata*s—we find a certain consistency in action and intent, a link between ideas and living, between what women do and what they say. The rituals form and express the relation between the world of daily action and the concept and ideas concerning women on their own and in the wider society. The rituals carry symbolic meanings which can be understood through the performances as well as through the exegeses given by women. The rites center around the world of married women's daily lives, particularly the precautions that express a basic principle of opposition in Bengali life: purity and pollution. In order to create and maintain purity—of the household, of the cooking area, of one's person, of the meals one eats, of the people around one, of one's relatives, kin, and caste group—rituals must be performed.

Besides announcing the start of a marriage to the gods and the ancestors, the marriage *strī ācār*s signify something to the household, local caste group, neighborhood, and all one's relatives by blood and marriage. The *strī ācār*s are the first signs of marriage, the first set of rituals that set the stage for the induction of an outsider into the household. The rites publicize a couple's new stage of life, conceived of as the beginning of a journey (*biyer jātrā*).

Marriage is seen as a journey to a new locality, status, role, position, way of conduct—a new set of relationships. Bride and groom are reborn as husband and wife. Just as the newborn child's link to his mother is cut and he begins life as a continuation of his father's line, so the bride's tie to her father is cut so that she may journey to a new place and a new life. She leaves the status of virgin to become a wife. *Biye* as exemplified in the *ācār*s is an expression of married life for male and female, the expectation of fulfilling a sacred duty to the gods (*dharma*) and ancestors as well as to the community of the living. The rites highlight the severance of a married woman from her father's house and the tying of a wife (*strī*) to a new environment in her in-laws' house.

The Cultural Construction of the Category *Wife*

Medhatithi, a philosopher and commentator on sacred texts (A.D. 825–900), compares a wife with the Goddess of Wealth, a comparison still made by Bengalis. In a telling passage he states that a house without a wife is similar to one without wealth. For another sage, Kulluba, a wife brings blessings to her house and to her people when she frees her husband from his debt to the ancestors by bearing him a son. Manu, the sacred lawgiver, does not contemplate equality between women and men in his Commentaries on Women: "His ideal is that of oneness of the two and not of equality with each other" (Das, 1962: 41). Men and women are each allotted different duties and rights which they have to fulfill in a complementary way in the social and symbolic scheme of things. Women have their roles in the world of men; and in the world of women, men act as guests, gods, and husbands according to roles defined for them by women.

In Bengal, the very idea of auspiciousness, or blessedness, is associated with marriage and married women. A new wife (*strī*) is introduced to her husband's house as a deity, wife, and future mother. *Strī,* a term carrying a sacred meaning, not only denotes one's own wife but also stands for Lakṣmī (Goddess of Wealth), Durgā (the Mother Goddess), femaleness, motherhood, and womanliness. Newly married women are called Lakṣmī *bou*—a model of Lakṣmī, the embodiment of the goddess's qualities. (Lakṣmī *baṇgśa* is the deity of wealth of the male line.) Lakṣmī *bou* or *meye* (wife or daughter) signifies several levels of meaning: among Lakṣmī's qualities and values are the deification of thrift, order, and the use of nature's gifts (Das, 1962: 8–9); furthermore, Lakṣmī is symbolic of wealth, the wealth that a married woman brings to her husband's house and the wealth of giving birth to a child (*santān*). The kinship ties created by marriage are also looked upon as a form of wealth.

Although the new wife is looked on as a deity, the rituals performed at the welcoming ceremony reflect the concern of the women (and the men) for her as one who will "continue" a line but who may also "destroy" it. As Harita, an ancient sage, tells it:

> One must guard his wife against sensual contact, as the ruin of the wife involves the ruin of the family, the ruin of the line involves the ruin of all offerings to gods and Manus, the ruin of offerings involves the ruin of the soul, and the ruin of the soul means the loss of all the things (Das, 1962: 8–9).

Manu similarly explains how the purity of the offspring is secured by guarding the wife: " 'The husband himself, after conception, becomes an embryo and is born again of her. So as the male is to whom a wife clings, so even is the son whom she brings forth; let him, therefore, carefully guard his wife in order to keep his offspring pure' " (Das, 1962: 8–9). The quotation alludes to the notion of conception that I have already mentioned, a woman being the vehicle, carrier of the seed in her womb. The seed (issue) is kept pure through the purity of the woman. Thus a woman is by extension also the carrier of the line's purity and status. She reflects her husband's household, and the line's respect (*sammān*) in society, caste, and kinship groups. Men guard their wives' actions and protect them from actions deemed injurious (commensality, sexual contact, bad company) so as to guard at the same time their own purity and that of the line and the ancestors. A woman must always remain chaste (*pativrata*) and pure: "In the Dharmasastras strict fidelity and devotion to the husband are stressed as the guiding principles of a woman's life" (Kapadia, 1966: 173).[18]

To prevent the pollution of a house and a line, brides have to be familiarized with their in-laws' codes of action. Wives are to model themselves on their mothers and mothers-in-law. As children, girls prepare for marriage by performing Śiva *brata* (worship to secure husbands like the Lord Śiva). Brides are like Lakṣmī and are also meant to be like Savitri, patient and devoted to their husbands and mothers-in-law. For the incoming wife, complete submission to new rules and to laws of the house must be placed above any private goals that may be contrary to those of her in-laws. She is to have no goals of her own beyond those of the wider group (house, family, or caste-kinship group). The ideal wife reflects a desire for life devoid of quarrels, tension, and hostility.

Even in Vedic times the ideas of the household and line were well established with the father as the head. Laws of marriage were recognized, and definite rites and ceremonies of marriage were observed. Marriage was the induction of a wife into the house, and with this the inmarrying woman acquired new duties and responsibilities. The responsibilities of the house and of the wife were so integrally related that the wife stood (as she does today) for the *paribār*—the house together with everyday life. Today as well, the status of the male members in a house is directly reflected and determined by the women's statuses, roles, and codes for conduct. The code of conduct to which a bride must conform includes norms of behavior, standards of action, and rules of the house which restrict movement inside and outside the household compound. She is expected to act like a *boumā* even before the marriage is consummated on the fourth day of the rituals. Immediately after marriage, the bride begins to act out her new roles of wife, mother, and older sister. These roles include accommodating herself to the various members, different generations, and kinship ties in the household through prescribed ways of acting and expressing sentiments. The bride is a mother to the very young children (HBS/D) in the house. She is also a mother in relation to children of other "mothers," such as her HBW, whose brother (HBWB) in turn becomes, by extension, the bride's children's *māmā* (MB) and to whose children in turn the bride is a mother. As a mother who will care for, feed, clothe, and protect the children of the house, a bride's relation to her HBW is that of sister. The link between *jā* (HBW) being a reciprocal one, there is no emphasis on inferior or superior roles. Rather, the accent is on equality and amity between women who are strangers to the house and often to each other. New brides accept their menial labor as befits them, receiving their instructions from mothers-in-law and the rest of the elder members of the house with humility and dignity. Mothers-in-law assign work to their sons' wives: except for occasional supervision, they themselves almost never take part in the work.

Here we can see why a new wife is visualized as a fish out of water—cool, calm, and motionless. The fish also stands for wealth and is a symbol of Lakṣmī. In addition, a bride is likened to a new stalk of rice (*dhān*) which is tender and auspicious—and again a symbol of Lakṣmī. Urquhart writes in her study of Hindu women: "When the milky substance first appears in the swelling ears of rice the cultivators make an offering of *sādh* (good thing to eat), such as is given to expectant mothers in the ninth month of pregnancy, while they sing, 'Mother Lakṣmī . . . has entered the womb of rice.'" (Urquhart, 1925: 9). Similarly, a new wife enters the womb of the *baṇgśa* through the change of *gotra* status and subsequently produces children for the line. In fact, the "womb of rice" and "womb of women" are reflections of each other. The central theme is simple and clear: women are carriers, vehicles for the male seed. The male line (and seed) is encompassed by the woman's womb, and like the milky substance which appears in ears of rice (a sign of maturity) the fluid of the womb also ripens. The birth of a child is analogous to the ripening of fruit (*phol*) and the harvesting of produce.

Women's rituals stress these ideas of woman as container of earth, man as seed, and male in female as seed in the earth. Sitā, wife of Lord Rāmā (the god-king of the Rāmāyana), was born of the earth and rose out of the earth's furrow; hence the reference in rituals to the new wife as Sitā. The husband is idealized as Śiva, the male god par excellence. According to the Rāmāyana, when Rāmā rejects Sitā for her supposed infidelity, Sitā's mother (the earth) takes her back after her marriage to Rāmā. Wives liken themselves to earth (*māṭi*), emphasizing their nature as bearers of children. Women are the sperm bearers, and males are the sperm itself. Sperm, *bīj* (seed), is culturally defined, embodying male descent and male-linkedness.

Women outside the line are the only means through which men can bring about their own immortality. A woman bears children in her womb, but the child is that of her husband. Like the tender rice stalk, the young bride and the expectant mother is divinized, for her power to create or destroy the line. According to Medhatithi, a woman is like the earth because both are capable of bearing burden (fruit) (Das, 1962: *passim*). As a part of the marriage ritual the mother of the bride or groom drags the *ācal* of the *sāri* on the ground to collect dust—earth—for its sacred and auspicious qualities, the dust of the street being mother earth herself. This notion of women carrying and containing is central to my Chapter 1 discussion of conception and birth.

CONCLUSION

The activities of women in Bengal form a social domain separable and understandable in its own terms. This domain is not defined by morphology alone (i.e., by separate sex-role activities). Rather, the domain of a woman's society is defined and interpreted in relation to the society at large by the cultural dimension of social action—the set of meanings expressed through symbols and categories. Bengali women's domain is rendered visible, systemic, and coherent, is constituted as well as expressed, by the rituals performed by women alone, rituals which provide an intrepretation of a social domain when analyzed through indigenous cultural categories. Women's rituals and structures separate women as a group and at the same time link them to the society as a whole. In turn, the rituals of marriage and the symbolism of femaleness and womanhood in these rituals contribute to an understanding of caste and kinship in a hierarchical society.

By studying women we have come full circle to a consideration of hierarchy and complementarity in caste society: the same general principle of hierarchy that Bougle (1971) and Dumont discuss but from a different perspective. Women do act in a separate domain in Bengal, and they express the meanings of this domain through rituals. But being separate does not mean being isolated; neither does it mean that the women's world is not subject to hierarchy. On the contrary, an examination of the nature of this separation yields a fuller understanding of a complementary and hierarchical relation between women and society. The women's domain is itself an encompassed element in Bengali hierarchical society.

Women in Bengali society are either wives of a line or daughters of a line; marriage establishes women as wives, and birth makes them into daughters. As a corollary to this and in my attempt to resolve the ambiguity in the position of women in relation to caste society, I have pushed the inquiry to a consideration of indigenous ideas concerning the theory of conception, marriage, and ritual. The merit of this approach is that it sheds light on the position, role, and the status of women in a Hindu society. The cultural construction of the person and the many levels of meanings in the concepts of blood and *gotra* further clarify the distinction between relatives and categories of relatives.

Through rituals, married women define and interpret the separate world of women, a world with its own hierarchy and meaning and ideology in day-to-day interactions. Yet, at the same time, women emphasize through the rituals the complementarity of male and female as these relate to the indigenous principles of female and male divine power. Through rituals women enact the actual and expected roles of virgin, daughter, wife, daughter-in-law, mother, and mother-in-law. The rites not only enact and express reality but represent the reality itself as women conceive of it and as society relates to it. Women's concerns with the *saṇgsār,* conception and birth, the status of married women, the wealth of the house and the gods of the line, neighborhood, and caste groups are all parts of women's rituals. Furthermore, the women's symbolism and women as symbols of the rituals are both tied to the ideas, aims, and motivations of performing *brata*s and *ācār*s. Symbolizations of women as "containers," "holders," "vessels," "carriers" are not only expressed but constituted and formed in the rituals. The rites themselves maintain, create, and set the boundaries of the women's social world. They parallel Hindu mythologies in that the principles of *puruṣ* and *prakriti* are expressed and accomplished by the gift of a virgin in marriage.

Through the symbolism of marriage, Bengali married women emphasize the sacredness and meaning of the male and female union as this union is brought about by complex rituals. The meaning of alliance (*ādān pradān*) as established by the marriage link is clearly manifested in the giving of gifts to one's *kuṭum* and *jñati.* The manner of giving and the nature of the gift elaborate the relationships within the kin and alliance domains through the complete series of women's rituals.

The sociological meaning of marriage, the husband-wife tie, the complementarity of femaleness and maleness, the household relations (especially those introduced and taught to an incoming bride), and the code of conduct of one's father and father-in-law are clearly enacted and symbolized in the rituals. *Strī ācār*s express the joining or severing of relationships between a bride and the two houses in her life. The rituals not only express, but are the *process of,* joining or severing relationships. *Ācār*s at the bride's house introduce her to household concepts of women as wives and mothers and to concerns of women regarding female power, and procreation. *Ācār*s in the in-laws' house introduce the bride to her new code of conduct, to the role of a daughter-in-law, and to her position in a new society of women.

The incoming women of a line share in the management and running of the *saṇgsār,* consisting of the members of one's house and their lives. This includes activity within the house (the physical location), the domain of affectivity, kinds of relationships obtained among relatives, links with servants, and care of the animals within the compound. Providing for members of a house, old and young, servants, priests, and other *jajmān* is a part of everyday work. Marriage, death, and birth are a part of the *saṇgsār. Saṇgsār* ties are ongoing, enduring, reciprocal, and dependent (Fruzzetti and Östör, 1976a). They encompass locality, relatives, and sentiments.

By examining the varied exchanges and cultural construction of gifts as well as the meanings in the rituals of giving and receiving, one sees that gifts and prestations in Bengali society yield many meanings and symbols. I have emphasized the unidirectional nature of the gift: prestations accompanying the bride create an imbalance between a woman's *śvaśur bāṛi* and *bāper bāṛi.* The former receives and rarely gives; the latter bestows gifts continually and rarely receives (except in cases of an exchange marriage or a reversal in the direction of marriage).

The Bengali conceptualization of the ideal woman is a married woman. By contrasting females in their unmarried, married, and widowed states in relation to auspiciousness and inauspiciousness, positive and negative aspects of *śakti,* "good" and "bad" power of femaleness, one sees the importance of marriage and ritual in Bengali society.

The gift of a virgin is a father's greatest gift to his newly acquired relatives. This gift links lines, houses, and groups of people into an ongoing system of exchange whereby houses further give or take daughters in marriage (or terminate the relationship with the one gift itself). The gift of a virgin guarantees the purity of one's line and the purity of one's women. The Bengali alliance system (*ādān pradān*) is unique in its absence of concrete and enduring groups to whom one constantly gives or from whom one constantly takes women in marriage. Furthermore, there is neither a terminological nor a hypergamous subordination of one pair over the other: the terms for HF/M and WF/M emphasize equality and reciprocity between the givers and the receivers of the woman. As far as the terminology is concerned, all marriage-linked categories of persons in the same generation become blood relations in the following as well as the preceding generations.

The principles of purity and pollution in relation to women express the status and position of woman in the hierarchy within the women's domain. Marriage is an important rite of passage for women. Since women can only achieve completion of their self through a husband, it is in the opposition to a widow that the auspiciousness of a married woman most clearly emerges; married women have the highest position in the hierarchy of women; widows, the lowest. Here, highness and lowness parallel auspiciousness (married status) and inauspiciousness (widowhood). Marriage unites, death separates, and birth continues ties among relatives through women's rituals and symbolic action.

Gifts of one affine to another establish the ritual inequality of the bride-givers to the bride-takers in the alliance tie: even after the gift (*dān*) of a virgin one keeps giving gifts to one's D, DH, DHM/F, and DHZ/B. The unidirectional giving of gifts by the bride's father does not, however, carry over into an arrangement of concrete groups of relatives superior and inferior to each other; exchange and reversal marriages *are* possible in Bengal. Thus, the ritual of marriage itself establishes an inequality (bringing with it a unidirectional flow of gifts) but does not arrange the whole society into ranked groups on the basis of hypergamy.

The *paona* and its relationship to caste hierarchy is parallel to the ritual of *bou bhāt,* where cooked rice is served and offered to one's caste relatives as a *paona* for accepting the bride as an equal. In caste hierarchy, the Brāhmaṇ, the washerman, barber, and drummer are given gifts. Ritual acts of purification are performed to objects (hearth, barber's kit, drum). The receivers of the *paona* perform their services just as they do in everyday life in the *jajmani* system. The *jajmān/kamin* (patron/client) tie is reinforced on this auspicious day, for *jajmani* services are especially required on this day and without them the marriage festivities are incomplete. Brāhmaṇs act as cooks preparing pure cooked food which all castes may consume together. In the context of the *strī ācār*s the barber's touch is auspicious and removes pollution, creating purity in the *strī ācār*.

The *bou bhāt* is a direct acknowledgment of equal status. Accepting cooked food—especially cooked rice—creates equality in a hierarchical society between the statuses of the bride and (by extension) those of her father-in-law's lines. To refuse cooked food is in itself a direct reflection of a refusal to accept equality. Eating the food offered (a *paona* in itself) is the gift one receives for the acknowledgment. Food is the medium through which the bride is introduced to her husband's caste fellows and the society at large. Only after thus having made the bride fully one's own can the marriage itself be consummated.

The bride pays her respects to her in-laws through the *praṇāmi* gifts. The receivers of the gifts accept her as one of their own. The cooked food of *bou bhāt* and the gifts are also parallel: in the former the local caste groups acknowledge the bride as an equal in caste status; in the latter the bride is accepted by the women of the house as a wife of the male line. Male/female complementarity is here shown by the importance of both sexes in relation to the bride. Men welcome the bride into the caste group, and women bring her into the line (which is in turn encompassed by caste). This accommodation and acceptance is achieved through the symbolism and meaning of gifts in Bengali society.

To maintain and continue the purity of the line and ensure and maintain the harmony of the *saṇgsār,* a wife must be introduced into her in-laws' social system. The relationship of the *ginnī* to the incoming bride is specified on the first day of the bride's arrival. The *ginnī*'s role in the preservation of the family's honor and prestige through her selection of a daughter-in-law and in the allocation of different occupations to each woman in the house makes her occupy the highest position in the hierarchy of women. Hers is a central and sacred role in *saṇgsār.*

Wives of a line are welcomed as deities and accepted as equals by caste members and as *āttiya*s by in-laws. In the rituals, the bride invokes her new ties with her in-laws by accepting a low position in the house. The bride in return is accepted and initiated to a new role as wife and mother although she has an inferior position among her in-laws until she bears her first child, after which her position and status in the house again change. After giving birth, she is considered to have fulfilled her *dharma.*

Married women journey back and forth between father and father-in-law's houses, reminiscent of the Goddess Durgā's annual autumnal journey to her father's house enacted at Durgā *pūjā* (the festival of the Goddess Durgā). Married daughters enter their father's house and depart to their husband's residence as deities. After marriage the brother-sister tie likewise continues. A brother's house becomes one's children's maternal house. The relationship between a *māmā* (MB) and *bhagna/bhagni* (ZS/D) is a very special one both in sentiment (affectivity) and ritual. The roles of a *māmā* are clearly marked in all the life cycle rituals and, in effect, continue the married woman's social and ritual ties with her father and all the persons of the father's ancestral line.

A married woman mediates between the two houses, the two lines, and in the creation of new lines. The *kanyā kañjali ācār* beautifully enacts and symbolizes a married woman's position between the two houses: blood ties with one's father and brother are not broken by marriage, yet the bride joins a new line to produce children for that line and not for her own ancestral line. Married women take their dormant *mātṛ śakti* to their father-in-law's house, where it is activated by the husband (male seed, male blood). The same bride does not and cannot offer her father's blood (male *rakta*) to her father-in-law's line; she retains that within her, continuing the relationship between herself and her father's male-line relatives. As a mother, a woman passes her *mātṛ śakti* to her children; the male blood of her father ends with her death.

Marriage relates all aspects of exchange—sacred, economic, and kinship—that effect, separately and together, the alliance between different lines. But marriage does not single out any one aspect of these exchange relationships as being either the primary, basic, or determining one. The social and economic positioning of the houses negotiating the marriage is achieved by the dowry settlement of the alliance. The marriage ritual itself is the sacred aspect, symbolizing the creation of a separate, sacred, ritual reality in addition to the inequal gift-giving relationship in the alliance. The acceptance of the sacred gift necessitates the giving of a second gift, the dowry, which in turn brings about the continuing link between the two lines through further prestations. The alliance relationship continues even if no other women are exchanged, since the prestations reaffirm the links among *kuṭum* and *jñati* relatives. At the same time, the possibility of further bride exchanges is secured and asserted. Having recognized equality through the exchange of a woman between two lines, the dowry complements status in the matching of lines. Here one can see the complementarity of hierarchical status and economic power in marriage alliance. The size of the dowry presents the economic power of the house and reflects the status of the bride (which parallels that of the groom).

One gains a greater appreciation of the concepts of purity and pollution by analyzing the network of relations among kinds of relatives in marriage rituals and in the *saṇgsār* action (women and the household being the most susceptible to impurity). The notion of hierarchy within household, kinship, caste, and locality groups is verified and defined by seeing what roles are performed among the family members and by observing how these groupings apply outside the household. Arrangements of marriage, the role of the daughter-in-law in the house, the division of labor within the *saṇg-*

sār, the introduction of a new code for conduct, and the possibility of future alliance with one's *kuṭum* and non-*jñati* relatives are expressed in the women's rituals—especially those at marriage.

The recent emphasis on and concern with change in the Indian family as it relates to marriage and women suggests that the family is being transformed from a unit of production into a unit of consumption and that the cementing bond of the family is being changed from one of extension to one of nucleation (D'Souza, 1970; Fonesca, 1963, 1964, 1966; Kannan, 1961, 1963; Kapadia, 1958; Kapur, 1970; Ross, 1961). Women are said to be breaking away from family control and family rules for behavior in favor of a self-regulated code for self-expression (D'Souza, 1970). These studies of urban women conclude that an emerging secular family (in contrast to the traditional and sacred family) will provide the model for future Indian families. Nevertheless, life in the rural or village context shows how tradition can coexist with change without contradiction, since change itself is constantly being redefined and understood in traditional terms. Although there is evidence of change at some levels, there is some resilience in hierarchical society. Marriage and ritual preclude drastic changes in the structure of the society. Today, the individual still accepts the assigned roles in the system of hierarchy and fulfills his or her obligations in the *saṇgsār*. Individual goals remain those of the house and line: the continuity of the present with ancestors; the maintenance of ties with *bhāiyat, jñati, baṇgśa*, and *kuṭum* through rituals and participation in the major life cycle rituals; and the group's code of conduct.

Studying women in the context of their own activities yields a domain in local, cultural terms. Women's rituals not only symbolize or express women's roles in society but are, to a large extent, *the* domain of action applying specifically to women. Women's rituals are a reality in themselves, not just a representation of something else. *Strī ācār*s not only symbolize women in Bengali society but also define, interpret, and form a women's world in its own right. Furthermore, the *strī ācār*s provide the mechanism by which women in roles and groups relate to the rest of a hierarchical society. Finally, the analysis of rituals shows the separation and complementarity of women in relation to men in Bengali society. Women are neither cut off from nor equal to men in the society as a whole; women are both encompassed by and complementary to man in the concept of the person, the constitution of lines and houses, the meanings of relationships among relatives, the construction of caste-kinship groups, the indigenous understanding of hierarchy, and the idea of a male/female relatedness. In the very understanding of hierarchy as given by the significance of marriage in Bengali society, women form one of the culturally understood elements. Women understand, interpret, and symbolize their world—the meaning and significance of their lives—through *strī ācār*s and *brata*s: a domain of actions separate from, and yet complementary to, the world of men.

Appendixes

Glossary

Notes

Bibliography

Index

APPENDIX A

Brahmanical Rituals

The rituals performed by the Brāhmaṇ priest at a Hindu marriage ceremony parallel and complement the women's rituals. The main parts of the marriage ceremony performed by the priest are the invocation of deities and the Seven Steps of Marriage (*saptapadi*). First, the priest invokes deities in various objects, asking them to come and participate in the marriage ceremony and to bless the couple. Second, the priest invites the ancestors to attend the marriage, to witness the union, and to bless the marriage. The aim of the marriage is to continue the line by producing a male child, who will make offerings to the departed ancestors. The last part of the marriage rituals is the actual binding together of the couple through the rite of the Seven Steps.

The gods invoked at marriage are directly related to the notions of wealth, the bearing of children, longevity, and immortality. The deities themselves are invoked in pairs, male and female, the attributes of the couples complementing each other. The sacredness of marriage derives from the priest's performance, in which he follows the sacred texts.

As soon as the *strī ācārs* are performed by the women the priest begins his worship. The first deity to be invoked is Basu Dhārā, the deity of the earth. Basu Dhārā is also known as Mother Earth, a deity who is invoked at all life cycle rituals. Basu Dhārā is also called *āmāder nāṛi Lakkhi-batso Lakkhi,* "our own Lakkhi, one of us, through the umbilical Lakkhi cord." Women say that Basu Dhārā is first to be worshipped because she is a part of the Mother, the Universal Mother Goddess. Earth is sacred to the Hindus, for Sitā, the wife of Rāmā, was born out of the earth and goes back into it. Women conceive of themselves as earth (*khettra*).

Nonetheless, the deity's manifestation is represented not as earth but by a drawing on the wall, since this is the form in which the deity wants to have her worship done. (Unlike Lord Kuber, the male counterpart of this deity, Basu Dhārā is not invoked into a clay pot.) The figure of the deity is drawn on the wall using a turmeric-colored cloth, cowrie shells, and cow dung. (The same representation is used for the Goddess Ṣaṣṭhī at birth rituals.) The priest draws the figure on the wall, using vermilion paste. The top part of the drawing is known as the auspicious person (a sign known as *putulikā*), a figure one finds drawn on the outside walls of the houses at auspicious times such as festivals and marriages. The priest is assisted in the drawing and invoking of the deity by the groom's or the bride's father, both rituals being performed separately at each of the two houses. The groom's or the bride's father stands against the wall, and the priest marks a spot representing the guardian's navel on the wall. Then the rituals continue as the priest pours seven strips of *ghī* (clarified butter), called *dhārā,* from the marked spot downward, and the mother of bride or groom makes sure that the butter does not touch the ground by holding her *ācal* against the wall. After the ritual of invocation is over, the mother places the *sāri* to her son's or daughter's head, thus imparting the deity's blessings. As the final act of the ritual, the priest hands the guardian a flower to offer to the bride's mother, which the father later places on the cow dung.

The male counterpart of Basu Dhārā is Lord Kuber, who is the guardian of wealth, whereas Basu Dhārā is the giver of wealth. The two roles parallel those of a man and a woman in relation to each other, the man protecting and housing the wealth, which is in fact the woman, who in turn gives wealth in the form of children.

Kuber is invoked into a small clay pot containing water. He has no actual figure or drawing to represent him except a clay pot filled with water in which he manifests himself. Three cups on a small wooden plank contain unhusked rice, fried rice, and water, all of which are symbolic of wealth in one form or another. Kuber's place of worship is set up in the storeroom, and his presence in the house is felt through the three days of the marriage. A small oil lamp is kept lighted during all this time, and if the light goes out, only the priest can light it again. Women can only add to the oil in the lamp, not touch the lamp itself. Here again, the priest alone invokes the god through incantations and worship. Women will start and end a *strī ācār* by paying their respects to Lord Kuber. The bride and groom are brought to pay respect to him many times throughout the day of the marriage.

The other pair of deities invoked as a male/female pair are Ṣaṣṭhī/Markandiya, the former being the giver of children and the protectress of children; the latter, her husband, the keeper or guardian of the dead ancestors. That is why these two deities are invoked at the next marriage ritual, the ancestral worship of *nāndīmukh*. In this rite, four generations of the father's ancestors and three generations of ancestors on the mother's side are invoked and offered water—a way of worshipping them. The marriage is the only time when ancestors of the mother's side are given respect in worship. Again the rites are elaborate and long, lasting a couple of hours. Each of the ancestors is named, his title and *gotra* mentioned, with a full complement of recitations and *mantras*. The deities Ṣaṣṭhī/Markandiya are each given a *paona* (which the priest takes with him); and Lord Nārāyan, who is a form of Viṣṇu, is also invoked and offered clothes, which also go to the priest. Nārāyan is the deity who witnesses the marriage at the *āgni sakkhī* ritual.

Having invoked the deities and given offerings to the ancestors, the priest again acts as the ritualist in the last major part of the rituals, performed at night, the Seven Steps of Marriage.

1. *Subha dristhi*—the first auspicious glance between the bride and the groom in front of the *camlatalā* (rites and recitation performed by the priest).
2. *Māla badal*—exchange of garlands between the bride and the groom.
3. *Hātu pūjā*—knee *pūjā*, where the bride's father touches the groom and pleads with him to accept his daughter.
4. *Sampradān*—the gift of the virgin to the groom.
5. *Hasta bandana*—the clasping of the hands and the changing of the *gotra*.
6. *Sindūr dān*—the giving of vermilion to the bride by the groom.
7. *Āgni sakkhī*—*āgni*, the deity of fire witnesses, the marriage.

In all of these rituals, the priest follows the sacred texts. Sometimes either the father of the groom or bride or the mother of the groom or bride or both may take part.

APPENDIX B

The Order of Strī Ācārs

*Strī ācār*s are rituals performed by married women with living husbands. Generally, they accompany life cycle rites where women's ritual activities parallel those performed by the Brāhmaṇ priest for the same occasion, but the two sets of rituals are different. Diachronically, *strī ācār*s appear in the following manner: *ācār*s 1 and 2 are performed a few days before the actual marriage day; 3–12 are performed on the actual marriage day; and 13 and 14 are performed after the change of *gotra*.

1. *Ḍheki mugla,* blessing the rice-husking foot paddle.
2. *Khoi bhaja,* frying of the pulses, performed a day or two before the actual marriage day.
3. *Śaṅkha paṛāna,* wearing the conch-shell bangle, performed on the morning of the marriage day.
4. *Ḍhol mugla,* blessing the drum.
5. *Dābi mugla,* blessing the barber's shaving kit.
6. *Onan mugla,* blessing of the newly constructed hearth on the first day of the marriage.
7. *Gāe halud,* smearing and splashing the body with turmeric paste.
8. *Kalāi mugla,* blessing of the pulses.
9. *Kauṛe khelā,* playing the cowrie shells.
10. *Snān,* bathing rituals on the edge of the pond.
11. *Baran karā,* the first part of the welcoming rituals for the groom and his party, performed in the evening before the priest performs the marriage rituals.
12. The second part of the welcoming rituals, performed inside at the bride's house after the arrival of the groom—called *satas kathi.*
13. *Kanyā kañjali,* rituals of farewell, performed in the bride's house on the day the bride and groom depart to their house.
14. The second set of welcoming rituals, *prabes karā,* performed by the bride's new in-laws on her arrival to her new home.

The first two *ācār*s are performed before the actual marriage day, the day when all friends and relatives partake in the marriage festivities.

By the time *ācārs* 3–7 are completed, the Brāhmaṇ priest begins the *nāndīmukh* ritual to honor the ancestors and does *Kubi pūjā.* The bride and groom are brought to attend the concluding part of the ancestral worship before completing *kalāi mugla.*

With the ancestral *pūjā,* the priest concludes his morning rituals. He appears in the evening for the night rituals, the Seven Steps listed in Appendix A. He begins his performance after the women have completed their welcoming rituals of the groom and his party.

The next day, the women complete the bathing on the *śil noṛā* and the rituals of farewell (*kanyā kañjali*). With *kanyā kañjali,* the women on the bride's side have completed their *strī ācārs*. The last *strī ācār* is performed on the eighth day by the women on the groom's side.

On the arrival of the bride and groom at the groom's house, the rest of the *strī ācārs* (13 and 14) complete the marriage from the perspective of married women, leaving *aṣṭamaṅgala* ('blessing of the eighth') for the eighth day.

APPENDIX C

Sociological Studies of Indian Women

Since independence the position of women in Indian society has undergone changes as a result of social and political changes. According to recent work by social scientists, women in India have become emancipated and modern in contrast to their preindependence position, which was one of subordination and exploitation. Hate (1969), Kapur (1970, 1974), Misra (1968), and Thomas (1939, 1964) have, however, disregarded the position of women in the rural areas in their analyses of Indian women. Their treatment of Indian women seems completely divorced from Indian culture, that is, they treat Indian women outside the context of their indigenous culture and place them in a universal "modern" setting. These four authors make use of Western concepts such as "modernity," "emancipation," "independence," and "equality" in their analyses of Indian women without once attempting to define these terms in the Indian context. Their approach is limited to the study of women in a particular social class divorced from the wider, underlying cultural setting.

Anthropological studies of women's rituals, family roles, and community status as cultural domain and as social system would help to present a richer and fuller understanding of women. Current forms of cross-cultural comparison use the Western woman as the model of modernity, in contrast to the "traditional" woman of India, even though Indian women are considered in their own terms, in the context of their own society. The Bengali case poses a special problem precisely because the social and categorical divisions are different in Western systems of thought and meaning and yet familiar enough for the Bengali case to be easily dichotomized as: Women = Subordination, Oppression, Inferiority, and Domestic exploitation. Such assumptions are based on the vague use of concepts such as "westernization" and "modernization" as against "tradition" and "subjection." These terms need clarification before they are put to use in comparative work. A study of women in one Indian society may not only help clear up such fallacies but establish an approach to cross-cultural study of women in other societies.

It is not sufficient to remark that women have played a relatively passive role in the family hierarchy and that one can now notice subtle changes taking place in attitudes. We are not told why women's position has changed (if at all). What was the role of women before and how has it changed? How has the cultural construction of women's roles been transformed, and is the change superficial or structural (Cf. Gough, 1959: 23–24; Gupta, 1974; Srinivas, 1942; Yalman, 1962, 1963, 1967)? Gough's (1955) attempt to analyze women's initiation rites centers more on the psychological motivations for the rituals than on sociological understanding. As a result her study emphasizes the purely sexual aspects of the rituals. She ends on an inconclusive note: "Initiation rites are a symbolic defloration because of the items used in the rituals stressing phallic aspects as well as female fertility." She associates female defloration with a fear of incest with one's own mother since daughter and mother are equated. Her analysis becomes oedipal, concluding that the "virgin in this caste is sacred: it is ritually dangerous to take her virginity. My hypothesis is that this is so because the virgin is unconsciously associated with the mother, as a woman whom it is desirable to approach." I disagree with this conclusion. The fear of sex is not that of incest with the mother but with the whole line. Women can cause pollution affecting the line. Gough concudes "that the virgin is unconsciously associated with the mother as a forbidden sexual object rests partly on the fact that in these rites the girl is brought into association with Bhagavadi, the mother goddess of Nayars and Tiyyars" (Gough, 1955: 87). My disagreement comes primarily from the inadequacy of the analysis of birth, conception, menstrual and marriage rituals, and indigenous views of male and female relations. The presence of the Mother Goddess in these rites suggests a similarity to Bengali menstrual rites, where the deity and the virgin are one, conception being the tie between virginity, womanhood, and divinity. Other attempts at symbolic analysis of women's rituals insist on viewing these rites as elements in the Great Traditions of Hinduism and Islam rather than as a system of symbolic action beyond the trait separations of great and little traditions (Ellickson, 1972).

The urban/rural dichotomy in the study of Indian women is a rather recent phenomenon. Kapadia (1966) and Kapur (1970) discuss the role of the working woman in urban centers; Fonesca (1963, 1964) and Kannan (1961, 1963) study intercaste marriages in cities; and to mention a few, Ross (1961), Shah (1974), Kapadia (1958, 1966), Singer (1968), and Kapur (1970) analyze the dissolution of the joint family system as a result of pressures of modernization. Yet, I ask: how do people in society orient themselves in relation to women; how has the dissolution of the Indian joint family affected women's ties and women's roles in the household, the kinship domain, the alliance system of marriage, marriage rituals, and so forth?

Women constitute a separate subculture in the regional societies of India; they interact among themselves in a domain where they are householders and men are simply guests (the reverse being true in the society at large). The idiom through which this domain is expressed is the world of *brata* cult (for Hindu women) and *pīr* reverence (for Muslim women) and life cycle rituals (for both).

The world of women is separate from that of men though women are not necessarily subordinated to men, nor are they inferior or less equal. In this society (unlike that of the West), separation of the sexes is not "an expressed antagonism. Women's society traditionally has a complex social structure of its own. In it women organize, conduct and participate in a wide range of work activities, sociability and ceremonies at a distance from the world of men. To it they bring their own leaders, skilled specialists and loyal followers. The separate structure allows freedom of action for women, away from men" (Peters, 1968). Fallers and Fallers (1976) note that the above is true of Turkish women in rural areas, and I add that the Bengali case does not deviate much from this Middle Eastern model.

Women in Bengal do constitute an indigenously separate world of meanings and symbols; and because they are separate in this indigenous sense (in ways other than the Western separation of men and women), one can approach the study of women in their own right. Yet one must clarify the meaning of this separateness; and the social relations among women, the construction of the women's domain, is the task of this work.

By analyzing rituals of birth and marriage, one may deduce the cultural construction of person, the roles of male and female, women as mothers, men as fathers, and the relation of parents to children. Furthermore, the relation of ritual actions to the exegesis of symbols and the significance and meaning of roles and statuses, male or female, may emerge through such a study. Rituals surrounding the death of a married male highlight the positioning of widows in Bengali society, caste, and household in relation to other widows, married women, and virgins. Further, the question of widow remarriage (absolute celibacy of widows being the cultural model) clarifies the concepts of *gotra* and blood in relation to the male line and changes in the society of women.

There is an all-India model for marriage, a civilizational construct shared by all regional Indian societies despite variations of caste and language (see Dumont, 1966). This model of marriage is based on Brahmanic rituals, elaborated to varying degrees of complexity in the sacred texts. This shared ritual model is not a "sacred" element separate from social relations; rather, it enters into the cultural, symbolic and ideological construction of meanings surrounding the actions, persons, and groups involved in marriage systems and practices in different Indian social contexts. The marriage rituals (Srinivas, 1966a; Stevenson, 1926; Underhill, 1921) and practices brought together by marriage are related to the structuring of kinship and caste relations as well as the notions of person, relative, and kinsman.

GLOSSARY

Abahan	Ritual of welcome
Abibāhita meye	Unmarried woman
Ācal	The end half of the worn *sāri* (woman's clothing); the part of the *sāri* used to cover the head of a married woman
Ācār	A rite; a traditional observance; a custom
Ādān pradān	Bengali system of marriage alliance; giving and taking women in marriage
Adhikār	A right; a responsibility
Āgni sakkhī	Fire witness
Alpanā	A ritual drawing accompanying a specific ritual act
Āltā	A red lac dye used by women to color the sides of their feet
Aśauc	Pollution; impure, impurity
Āśīrbād	A blessing
Aṣṭamaṅgala	The auspicious ritual performed on the eighth day of the marriage
Āttiya	One's own people; a person with whom one shares something
Badal biye	Exchange marriage
Badha	Bad omen; obstruction; an inauspicious event
Baṇgśa	Line
Baṇgśa bali	Line of descent from ancestors
Bār jātri	The groom's party in wedding rituals
Bāṛi	House, household
Bāsar ghar	Room where the bride and groom spend the first night of their marriage

Bastra	Cloth; can be *sāri* or *dhoti*
Basu dhārā	A ritual drawing put on the wall of a worship room or on the door of the main entrance
Bel mālā	Necklace made of sacred wood-apple tree
Bhadra	Proper, genteel, respectful
Bhāi	Brother
Bhāiyat	[From *bhāi* (brother)] the group of people with whom one shares blood in a recognizable form (i.e., male to male)
Bhakti	Love; devotion; sacred love
Bidai	Farewell
Bidhobā	Widow
Bīj	Seed; semen
Biye	Marriage; sacred marriage
Bou bhāt	Wife-rice; the first rice cooked by a new bride
Boudī	Elder brother's wife
Boumā	Wife-mother
Brata	A form of symbolic ritual act; a vow; a contract between a person and a deity
Brata kathā	Legends, sayings, or stories relating to specific *brata* rites
Camlatalā	The altar where the marriage rituals take place
Dābi	A rightful claim of a gift
Dādu	Father's father; Mother's father
Dān	A gift
Dhan	Wealth
Dhān	Paddy; unhusked rice
Dharma	Duties, responsibilities in the daily life
Dhoti	Hindu man's dress
Eyo	Married women in the context of *strī ācārs*
Gabar	Cow dung
Gāe halud	Smearing the body with turmeric paste

Ghar	House; household; dwelling
Ghat	A vessel of invocation
Ghāt	Open edge of water where daily bathing, washing, and also ritual activities are done
Ghatak	A go-between for two prospective marriage partners
Ginnīmā	Female head of household
Gotra	Titles of seers, or *ṛṣi*, said to have originated in the distant past; constituting a maximal descent label
Grahaṇ	To accept
Gurujan	Elders
Homa	Sacred ritual fire
Iñdur māṭi	Earth dug out from a mouse's hole
Jā	Husband's brother's wife
Jajmān	Giver of *jajmani* service
Jajmani	A system of ritual giving and receiving of goods and services
Jāmāi	Son-in-law
Jāti	Kind; caste; a system of classifying people
Jerṭhot	Father's brother's son or daughter
Jeṭhā	Father's brother
Jñati	[Not group-based term] a person related to one in the male line; referring to ties that go beyond the *sātpuruṣ* and *sapiṇḍa*
Kājal latā	Collyrium holder
Kāmāno	The act of barbering, paring nails, applying *āltā*
Kāmonā	A desire; a wish
Kanyā dān	The gift of a daughter
Kanyā kañjali	The gift a bride gives to her elders
Kauṛe	Cowrie shells
Khettra	Field
Kosṭhi bicār	Astrologer's chart; a horoscope
Kula	Line, meaning both an attribute and a group

Kuladebatā	An ancestral deity; the deity that belongs to the male line
Kulsi	A jug used to haul water from the river or to store water in
Kumāri	A prepubertal girl; i.e., a virgin
Kuṭum	The people to whom one gives daughters in marriage and from whom one takes wives for one's sons, being people with whom one does not share blood
Lagna	(Astrological) moment
Lajjā samparka	Avoidance relationship
Liṅga	(Male) symbol of Śiva
Mā	Mother, also applied to the Mother Goddess
Madhur samparka	Sweet relationship
Majja	Bone marrow
Mālik	Owner; head; householder
Māmā	Mother's brother
Maṅgal	[see also *Mugla*] Blessing; auspiciousness; good
Mantra	Incantation; sacred formula
Māsī(mā)	Mother's sister
Māstoto bhāi/bon	Mother's sister's son/daughter
Mātṛ śakti	Sacred female (i.e.; mother) power
Meye	Girl; woman; female
Meyeder	Of women; belonging to the women's world
Mṛittaśauc	Pollution caused by death
Mugla	[colloquial for *maṅgal*] Auspiciousness; good
Nāndīmukh	A rite honoring ancestors
Nanod	Husband's sister
Nāṛi	Navel; umbilical cord
Nikaṭ āttiya	A near relative
Nisi	Water drawn from a pond or river before sunrise
Nitkanyā	A pre-pubescent girl
Niyam karan	Customs and laws regarding a code of conduct

Pabittra	Sacred; pure
Pāi	A rice-measuring pot
Pān	Betel leaf
Pāṇi grahaṇ	The acceptance of the bride's hand in the marriage rite
Paona	A gift; a bestowal; given for services rendered
Pāp	Sin
Pāṛā	Neighborhood
Paribār	Someone's family, wife, or domestic unit; the household
Paricay	Physical, social, and intellectual introduction of a child by his or her father
Paṭ	A painted image of a deity
Pātā	Leaf
Patra	Groom
Patri	Bride
Phol	Fruit
Piṇḍa	A mixture of cooked rice used in *sapiṇḍa*
Pisī(mā)	Father's sister
Pistoto bhāi/bon	Father's sister's son/sister
Pitṛ puruṣ	One's ancestors in the male line
Pon	Dowry; goods and money agreed upon and paid by the bride's side to the groom preceding the marriage ritual
Prajā	Receiver of *jajmani* service; literally, subject
Prakriti	Created world; nature
Praṇām	A respectful gesture whereby a junior symbolically or physically removes the dust from the elders' or superior's feet
Prānpratiśṭhā	The consecration of a deity; giving life to a deity
Pratiśṭhā	To establish; to set up
Prem	Conjugal love
Pūjā	An expression of honor and respect through rituals; a form of worshipping deities

Puruṣ(a)	The male principle
Rakta	A culturally defined category for the substance people share; a symbol for a relationship among people and groups of people; blood
Rakta āttiya	A blood relative
Śālā	Wife's brother
Śālī	Wife's sister
Samāj	Society; caste society
Sambandha	Relation specifically through marriage
Sambandhī	Brother-in-law
Sammān	Respect
Samparka	A link between persons; a relationship
Sampradān	The sacred gift of the virgin at marriage by her father
Samṣkāra	A sacred sacrament; a purificatory rite of passage
Saṇgsār	The world of everyday life
Śaṅkha	Conch shell
Śaṅkha paṛāna	Wearing of conch-shell bangles
Santān	Issue; child
Sapiṇḍa	One's relatives in the male line who offer *piṇḍa* to the same departed ancestors in the male line
Saptapadi	The seven steps a Brāhmaṇ bride and groom take in the marriage rituals
Sāṛi	Hindu woman's dress; an Indian national dress
Śāsuṛī	Mother-in-law
Sātpuruṣ	The seven generations of one's male ancestors who receive *piṇḍa* offering
Śauc(a):	Pure; purity
Śil noṛā	The mortar and pestle used daily to grind spices
Sindūr	Vermilion
Sissu	Issue; a child to a mother
Snān	Bath; a complete bodily dip in the water
Śrāddha	Death rituals

Sthāpan	To install; to establish
Strī	A married woman; female in opposition to male; a married woman with a living husband
Strī ācār	A married woman's ritual
Śubha	Holy, pure
Śuddhatā	Pure; holy; sacred
Śvaśur	Father-in-law
Swāmī	Lord; husband
Tattva	Expected, anticipated gifts
Ululu	The ritual cry of women at *strī ācār*s and auspicious rites
Upahār	A gift given without any ritual context
Uttān talā	A plate containing 27 sacred items
Yoni	(Female) symbol of Śiva

NOTES

Introduction

1. In talking about society as a "whole" and the "wider society," I am not trying to give the impression of a rigid, static edifice; rather, I refer in a segmentary way to women in marriage rites and everyday life, to other groups in marriage relationships, to the town of Vishnupur and Bengali Hindu society as a way of categorizing levels. I use "Hindu society" and "Bengali caste society" interchangeably in discussing marriage groups, Vishnupur, and the region of Bengal. Muslim groups are not part of this study. I have written about Bengali Muslim rituals elsewhere (Fruzzetti, 1971, 1972, 1980a, 1980b).

2. The studies of Carter, Inden and Nicholas, Vatuk, David, Pocock, Van der Veen, and to some extent Dumont, treated women and women's rituals secondarily and perfunctorily as an aspect of the society at large, or worse, entirely ignored women as a social group. Pocock (1972: 96–97) devoted some attention to household and ritual, the ties between brother and sister, between mother's sister and mother's brother, and so forth.

3. This study of women and women's rituals cuts across the different residential sections of Vishnupur as well as the boundaries of class and caste. At the time of the fieldwork the town had a population of about 45,000.

Chapter 1: *Sampradān*

1. Marriage registration allows people to avoid other sanctions for not complying with the requirements of Hindu marriage. Registry marriages (whether or not they are in accordance with Hindu ideals) are linked to reforms of the inheritance system. Under the constitution of India as a secular state, these reforms allow intercaste and intercommunity marriages while guaranteeing property rights, since noncompliance with marriage rules could in fact result in one's being outcasted from one's own caste and kinship group.

2. In the winter of 1973 a well-founded rumor circulated in Vishnupur regarding a Brāhmaṇ girl who had run away to a nearby town to be married to a boy of the Sadgop (lower-ranking cultivating and trading) caste. Both were students at the local coeducational college. The news was not well received by a number of townspeople; some swore the couple would be thrashed if they ever came back to town.

3. The adoption was not ritually enacted; the boy and girl were simply brought up by the Brāhmaṇ women.

4. I deliberately use the term *line* for the Bengali *baṇgśa.* Lines are not "lineages" in the anthropological sense familiar to us as corporate groups for the African literature. "Lineages" would be erroneous here since *baṇgśa*s are not *patri* descent lines because they include the inmarrying wives, who *are* of the husband's line after marriage. I want to thank David Schneider for bringing this point to my attention.

5. *Thāk*s are also separated by purity and commensality rules, and they are ranked. The *gotra* prohibition of marriage has its functional equivalent among the lower *jāti* in the *baṇgśa* prohibition. Nevertheless, lower caste marriage differs precisely because the *gotra* is absent. This question, being part of a much wider problem of caste hierarchy, is reserved for a future work comparing the morphology of high and low *jāti*s.

6. The *ghāt* is the edge of an open body of water used for bathing and for washing clothes. Relatives who go to the *ghāt* are the *bhāiyat* in the most specific sense.

7. *Dharma* means duty or rule, and its generic use indicates all the duties and responsibilities a person has in everyday life according to his *jāti, baṇgśa,* and life cycle status formulated in Hindu ideologies and in the sacred texts.

8. *The Laws of Manu,* quoted in Kapadia, 1947: 222 and 142–143 respectively.

9. *Putrikā* from the Mitakshara, quoted in Tambiah, 1973a: 79–80.

10. For further information see Kapadia, 1947: 142–143.

11. Dumont, 1970a. "For modern common sense, hierarchy is a ladder of command in which the lower rungs are encompassed in the higher ones in regular succession" (p. 65).

12. At the birth of a male or female child, the midwife places the placenta in a brand new clay pot with seven or nine cowrie shells, one whole turmeric, and one betel nut (*supari*). A second clay pot covers the first one, and both are buried. Following this, a number of birth-related rituals are performed by married women only.

13. In one case I witnessed in Vishnupur, the prospective bride and groom belonged to different *baṇgśa*s (and *sapiṇḍa*) but had the same *gotra.* Since the union was much desired, the problem was solved by having a third house (of the same *jāti*) with a different *gotra* adopt the bride through an adoption ritual. This way the bride could change her *gotra* again in marriage.

Chapter 2: *Pon*

1. See Yalman's pioneering work (1962, 1967) on the purity of women in relation to caste boundaries in Ceylon and south India.

2. Here I differ from Tambiah's interpretation (1973a) of bride and dowry in marriage, where the two gifts are treated on an equal footing as gifts of a kind, both going in the same direction. Tambiah does not oppose dowry to bridewealth and states that the former can also be classed as a gift.

3. The responsible male and female elders of the house explore with great

care the question of whether the two negotiating houses are already related. There is no particular person in charge of this task.

4. Tambiah writes that "the 'gift of a virgin' accompanied by dowry appears to be associated with the ideal of monogamy, an ideal that is symbolized in the notion of a husband and wife being a united, inseparable pair which reached its ultimate elaboration in the institution of *suttee* (the widow burning herself on her husband's pyre) (1973a: 65)." In addition to monogamy, the factors to be considered here are caste status and purity of line, the status of women through the life cycle, and the hierarchy of male and female.

5. "One who gives the daughter should not receive anything" (Karve, 1965: 130).

6. "Alliance" has a different meaning in the context of anthropological studies in south India. See Fruzzetti, Östör, and Barnett, 1976.

7. Cf. hypergamy in the following works, where the direction of giving and the status of givers and receivers (as groups in a marriage circle) are both fixed: Inden, 1976; Pocock, 1972; Van der Veen, 1972; Yalman, 1967.

8. In one case I observed where an older, dark-complexioned bride was married to a desirable groom, a dowry of Rs.100,000 ($10,000) was paid. In this case, however, both houses were of high status and wielded considerable economic power.

9. Many new businesses are started every year. Most of them do not last more than a year. The question is important because a bride's father wants to know how the young couple will survive.

10. I have attended over 50 marriages in my three years of fieldwork.

11. For a more detailed discussion of matching lines, see Fruzzetti, Östör, and Barnett, 1976.

12. See Tambiah, 1973b; Vatuk, 1969, 1975. Dumont (1966) finds an alliance practice in the gift giving of north India which is similar to the south Indian principle. But alliance in the north is expressed through the prestations (linked to hypergamy), whereas in the south it is a kinship principle expressed in the terminological system itself.

13. For an extended analysis of Bengali kinship domain, see Fruzzetti and Östör, 1976a and 1976b.

14. The *bāsar ghar* is the room where bride and groom spend the night, entertained by *āttiya* and guests. The couple stay up all night to avoid the fate of Lakhindar in the myths of the Snake Goddess (where the groom died of snake bite during his wedding night).

15. Menstruating women cannot, however, participate in any of the rites.

16. In the same manner, a newborn has to wear a charm for six months to a year, after which he is free of the influence of uncontrollable spirits.

17. The intriguing question of who shaves the barber has a simple answer: another Nāpit caste person purifies his caste brothers. But the other barber has to be of a different *gotra* for the pollution to be removed.

18. The worst that can happen is missing the *lagna*, the astrologically calculated moment for the main ritual of the marriage. When this happens the whole set of rituals may have to be postponed to another day.

19. After each ritual during the marriage ceremonies, bride and groom

have to do *praṇām* to Lord Kubi. Having performed *praṇām* to Lord Kubi the bride's face is uncovered. The *ginnī* removes her *sāri*'s end (*ācal*) from their heads. They remain with Lord Kubi briefly and then depart for the next series of rituals.

20. Women may never utter their husband's name aloud. Should they do so inadvertently, they shorten the husband's life and have to fast that day in atonement.

21. Whole fish is an auspicious gift, a sign of wealth and prosperity. Fish are drawn in many contexts of marriage: on the ground as part of the *alpanās* (ritual drawings by women) and on the walls, buildings, pots, seats, and invitation cards. A whole fish is nailed to the main gate post as a symbol of auspiciousness and wealth, imparting good fortune to all the journeys associated with marriage.

22. During the first year of marriage the bride's father has to ask the *jāmāi*'s father to give the bride permission to visit him. The bride's father or brother then has to fetch the bride. All this is meant to express respect for the *kuṭum ghar.* After the visit the *jāmāi* is asked to escort his wife home and to allow her to come again. Also during that year, the bride-givers cannot eat in the bride-taker's house. When the year is over the young couple are invited, fetched, and feasted in the bride's father's house. After this feast, bride-givers can eat at the house of bride-takers.

Chapter 3: Betel Nuts, Cowries, and Turmeric

1. *Badha* is an obstruction of the good and the auspiciousness (*maṅgal kāmonā*) the ritual is supposed to produce. As such it is a reflection of some other trouble in the house, if only a neglect of the proper performance of rituals and propitiation of vengeful gods. A common *badha* rite is the feasting of an expectant mother in the ninth month of pregnancy. In this rite the woman eats nine varieties of cooked curry, sweets, fruits, and other good things. If a pregnant woman dies on this day, a house may abandon this custom altogether, fearing a repetition. The rationale is that the *ācār* may have "suited" the ancestors but does not suit their descendants. On the other hand, a *badha* of the ancient past may be lifted for the present generation and become once more auspicious. Another ritual may replace the discontinued one. A *badha* is a reflection of the danger and fear involved in life cycle rites. But in the case of pregnancy and birth, the passage (which the rituals surround) is itself dangerous and frought with potential evil, leading naturally to *badha* associations.

2. Widows (*bidhobā*) are excluded from *strī ācārs* because they represent a negation of the married state. A husband's death makes a widow inauspicious, rendering her ineligible to participate in auspicious occasions. The death of a husband is a tragedy for a woman, but even more important, the death of an only son may mean the end of a line.

3. This does not mean that I do not take into account the exegesis offered by the priest for the marriage rites as a whole. Rather, I treat all interpretations sociologically, in the context of action.

4. All these rituals are Brahmanic in nature, performed according to precepts set down in the Śāstras: Vedas, Smritis, and Grihasutras collected in the *Purohit Darpan.* For a list of such rituals see Carstairs, 1957; Stevenson, 1926; Underhill, 1921.

5. The lower castes have their own ritualists who act as priests, paralleling the actions of the Brāhmaṇ in relation to gods and goddesses.

6. Breaking conch shells is inauspicious because broken shells are associated with death of a husband. Married women's bangles come in pairs, so if one of a pair is broken ('gone cold,' *ṭhāṇḍā*) it has to be replaced soon after. Widows must break their conch shells and immerse them in water—a pond or a river—or bury them under the sacred tulsi tree.

7. Turmeric is a sacred food item often used for purifying objects as well as the body, for cooking, and for medicinal purposes. It forms the base of any cooked curry, being ground fresh for each meal. It appears in rituals as an item of offering for the gods. It is used to purify oneself after the period observed for birth and death pollution. Turmeric can also be smeared on the body at the daily bath. For curing skin disease and infections, it is smeared on the skin. Townspeople praise the "scientific" use, value, and purposes of turmeric.

8. The bride may receive conch shells from her in-laws' house, but the gift of such bangles is not followed by any special ritual. Actually, the bride may continue to wear the pair given by her in-laws, keeping the pair given by her father intact for one year.

9. Babies wear the end piece of the conch shell (*padak*) up to six months after birth. The *padak* acts as a safeguard against evil spirits during this time. Here the shell stands for Mother Ṣaṣṭhī (the Goddess of Children). The newborn is in danger of spirits until six months after birth.

10. After one year she can wear it without the fear of tearing it. The *sāri* is a gift from her father (*bāper dān*).

11. Iron is used to fend off evil spirits (unfriendly ghosts who roam the air and spiritual beings who wish evil and want to harm persons at the most auspicious moments of their lives). Objects made of iron are therefore used for life cycle rites such as birth and marriage. Iron rings, bangles, and arm bands are used in other contexts for similar ends.

12. The significance of iron is recounted in the myths of Manasā, the Snake Goddess. In the marriage of Lakindar and Behulā there is a room made of iron (*bāsar ghar*) where bride and groom spend their first night keeping vigil to avoid evil and bad influence. See Dimock, 1969, and Dimock and Ramanujan, 1964.

13. Whenever an auspicious work (*śubha kāj*) is about to be performed, turmeric is invariably one of the items used in the performance. Even the invitation cards sent out to invite people for the marriage are lightly smeared with turmeric and vermilion on one side. Turmeric spots (*akar*) are placed on the *ācal*s of the *sāri*s given as gifts for the marriage to *kuṭum* or *jñati.* It is after the application of turmeric to the groom and bride that women insist on no one—especially widows and spinsters—touching the couple.

14. The everyday use of grinding stone and pestle (*śil noṛā*) is to prepare spices for the main meal of the day. The stones are washed every day and

fresh spices are placed on the flat *śil;* the cylindrical *noṛā* is used to crush the whole turmeric, onions, hot peppers, ginger, garlic, and pepper. After use, the stones are washed again. The *śil* is stood upright against the wall and the *noṛā* is placed next to it. The two stones are never separated; always together, they express the mother-child tie—hence the representation of the Goddess Ṣaṣṭhī by the *śil noṛā* in the rituals of Ṣaṣṭhī.

15. The use of cowries as money in the past is still recalled in certain rituals. If a child is born under an auspicious star, his father will "sell" him or her to another caste and the payment is done in cowries. The "sale" of the child is a symbolic gesture; the child remains with his parents. Cowries also represent children; they stand for the deity Ṣaṣṭhī, the Goddess of Children, as well as Lakṣmī, the Goddess of Wealth. Cowries are used to make the statue of the deity Ṣaṣṭhī at birth rituals.

16. It is my thesis that Lakṣmī and Ṣaṣṭhī are a single female divinity, aspects of which are projected as one or the other goddess in specific circumstances. This is made clear in the *basu dhārā,* the invocation of Kuber and Ṣaṣṭhī/Markandiya.

17. The principles of *puruṣa/prakriti* are also expressed in other contexts by the symbolism of *strī ācār*s in marriage. The oval-shaped *pān* stands for the *yoni,* and the whole betel nut is the *liṅga* in the *kalāi mugla* ritual. In the puberty rite of first menstruation the *yoni* and the *liṅga* are represented by the *śil noṛā, śil* being *yoni* and *noṛā* being *liṅga.* When the menstruating girl is secluded in a dark room for three days holding the *noṛā* (*liṅga*) in her lap, the girl herself is the *śil* (*yoni*).

18. I observed this form of welcome only in the marriage rituals.

19. This is also done when a new house is consecrated (*bāṛi pratiśṭhā*).

20. During the year there are four major festivals of Lakṣmī, but every Thursday Lakṣmī *pūjā* is done by the married women of the house. Women ask for wealth in these rites. At every Lakṣmī *pūjā,* a fish is invariably drawn on the floor of the worship room and outside the room as well. It is considered to be very auspicious to see a fish when making a journey to a new place or entering one's house.

21. The Goddess Lakṣmī is known to be calm (*santa*), peaceful. When children cough or cry, mothers say "Be quiet *Lakkhir cele,*" meaning "Try to be calm like Lakṣmī."

22. *Sindūr dān* in the Brahmanic rites is equivalent to wearing the iron bangle in the *strī ācār*s. Vermilion and iron bangle together represent married status and must come from the in-laws' house.

23. Married women and newborn babies stand in danger of departed spirits who may be destructive to them. The spirits out to destroy women with babies or the newly married are those of women who died in childbirth or during pregnancy or before marriage or first menstruation. Iron, being sacred and pure, strong and powerful, helps fend off evil spirits, who fear contact with it. Women therefore wear iron bangles for protection. The room of the newly married couple in the story of Behulā was made of iron. The Kāmār (the blacksmith) made the *bāsar ghar,* and this is the caste group which continues to make the iron bangles today. Women add that they also

wear the iron bangles because doing so is auspicious and good for one's husband.

24. Kārtik, the son of the Goddess Durgā, went back to the house after his *bidai* because he forgot to wear his crown. He never got married, for in the house he met his mother grieving at the loss of her son to another woman. Similarly, a bride should not look back when she leaves her father's house on the completion of *kanyā kañjali.*

25. The fruit of marriage (*biyer phol*) is the male child; the means of accomplishing this is amply expressed in the symbolism of marriage: like the *śil noṛā,* both the *pān* and betel nut, and the *ḍheki* structure and the *kājal latā,* represent the *liṅga* and *yoni* joined together. At marriage the bride takes with her the full use of her sexuality as she is given to her husband in the marriage.

26. Cow dung is also used at child birth for the same reason: that the newborn be cool and composed like *gabar. Gabar* is important for purification rituals. It is used to purify the ground; it is smeared on the earthen floor before the beginning of any sacred work. It is also used to purify objects used for rituals and utensils before they are used to store food.

27. There is a parallel between this bath and the *śil noṛā snān.* The former removes marriedness while the latter establishes it.

28. Married women in their in-laws' house will always be assisted at the *ghāt* by their own father's people even if the death in the house is not that of their husband. For any death within the whole house makes them impure, and the period of death pollution has to be observed and rituals have to be performed at the *ghāt.*

Chapter 4: Marriage and the Statuses of Women

1. Satapatha Brāhmaṇa, or "Belonging to Brāhmaṇs," are works composed by and for Brāhmaṇs. The works contain details of Vedic ceremonies, with long explanations of the origin and meaning of the rituals. The Brāhmaṇas abound with legends, divine and human. The Satapatha is the most complete, systemic, and important of the Brāhmaṇas. See Dowson, 1961: 286.

2. *The Laws of Manu,* quoted in Kapadia, 1947: 87.

3. See Dumont, 1970a, for a further elaboration of the Brāhmaṇ's position in the caste system.

4. See Gupta, 1974, for a similar approach.

5. The following acts of legislation for marriage are worth noting. By the Special Marriage Act of 1872 the British government sanctioned intercaste marriage provided that the couple declare no religious affiliation. In 1887, the Indian National Social Conference encouraged intercaste marriage between the subdivisions of the same caste. The conference also stated that castes which permitted interdining should also permit intercaste marriage. The Special Marriage Act as amended in 1923 enabled persons belonging to different castes to marry even if they declared themselves professing Hindus. In 1933, the Caste Tyranny Removal Act of the Baroda Government

and the Aryasamaj Marriage Validity Act legalized marriage among Arya-Samajists in British India. The Hindu Marriage Disabilities Removal Act of 1946 validated marriages within one's own *gotra* and marriage between sub-castes. The Hindu Marriages Validity Act of 1969 legalized and gave sanction to intercaste marriages. See Kannan, 1963: 198–199.

6. Hypergamous systems of a kind are present among the Anavil Brāhmaṇs; the Leva-Patidars of Gujarat; the Rajputs of Gujarat, Rajasthan, and Maharastra; and the Nayars, Kshatriyas, and Ambalavis of Kerala. See Sur, 1973: 17.

7. Kulinism was a custom in Bengal whereby a man married a girl of equal or slightly lower status within the divisions of the high castes. Rich families of somewhat lower rank hoped to raise their status by paying exorbitant dowries and marrying their daughters into Kulin families. A Kulin groom in turn could marry several wives. See Chakraborty, 1963; Dumont, 1970a: 120–121; Inden, 1976; Kapadia, 1966; Karve, 1965: 116–117; Majumdar, 1971.

8. The act of giving gifts serves a special role in society. As I have shown, gifts symbolically link two groups of people. In Mauss's analysis of such rituals, he defines both an obligation to receive (the inferior position) and an obligation to reciprocate (the superior position). This is not the case, however, in the sacred gift of a woman in Hindu marriage. On the contrary, the bride-givers are not superior to the bride-receivers. Bride-takers have the higher status in this relationship in Bengal, and they are under no obligation to reciprocate. See Mauss, 1967: 72.

9. Dowson defines *Smriti* as: "What was remembered, inspiration or direct revelation. In its wide-range application, it includes a number of texts, the *Vedangas*, the *Sutras*, the *Ramayana*, the *Mahabharata*, the *Puranas*, the *Dharma-sastras*, especially the works of Manu, Yajnawalkya, and other inspired law-givers, the *Niti-sastras* and its limited application relates to the *Dharma-sastras*; Manu says that *Smriti* means the institution of law" (Dowson, 1961: 301). See also Chattopadhyaya, 1964.

10. See the excellent study by Kapadia, 1947, which relates property to blood and rituals in an intriguing manner.

11. Hindus follow the Smriti rules (Law Books), also known as Dharma-sutras. "The Dharmasutra of Manu is the standard and most authoritative work on Hindu Law that presents the normal form of Hindu society and religion. The pivot around which the laws relating to marriage turned is the law of consanguinity as embodied in the conception of *sapiṇḍa, gotra* and *pravana*" (Sur, 1973: 59, 63).

12. For contrast see Vreede de Stuers, 1968, where the private domain of Muslim women is the household in clear opposition to every other domain. See also the studies on Muslim women by Jones and Jones, 1941; Khan, 1972; Khawaja, 1965; Niaz, 1929; Papanek, 1973; Siddigi, 1952. There is no such strict exclusion in Bengal.

13. Baig, 1958; Kapadia, 1958: 168. Here I want to repeat that Brāhmaṇ priests will not attend or perform the marriage rituals of the low castes. In a future work I will cover the question of low-caste kinship and marriage.

14. Bengali Muslim women undergo similar ritual activities before and

after marriage. These rites fall under *ādāt* (customary action). For Muslims, marriage is a contract in which the economic rights of a woman are guaranteed by the *mahr*, a sum of money settled upon by the husband at the time of the marriage ceremony. The husband is bound to give the *mahr* to his wife in case of a divorce. The religious significance and differences of marriage between the two communities have received a lot of attention. Islamic and Hindu beliefs are present even in the daily activities and life of both communities and account for the differences between the two groups.

15. Inden and Nicholas define *sapiṇḍa* as sharing the same body particle, and *jñati* as sharing one body, thus allowing two types of relationships: those who share "our body" and those who do not. Thus their analysis of the ambiguous position of women as wives and daughters of lines remains vague.

16. The notion of women as field is derived from my field research, but a similar idea based on textual sources has been independently developed by Tambiah: "An underlying distinction which acts as an axiom in the evaluation of mixed marriages is that between male 'seed' and female 'field' or 'soil' in the theory of conception. It is declared that between the two, the male seed is more important, but not exclusively so for 'seed sown on barren ground perishes in it,' while 'good seed, springing up in good soil turns out perfectly well' " (Tambiah, 1973b: 198, from a reading of *The Laws of Manu*, vol. 10, pp. 69, 71, 72). Here, then, the ethnographic use of the metaphor "field" for women parallels the conception of women in the sacred texts.

17. Whereas Wadley (1975) describes rites accompanied by the *kathā*, a verbal recitation, life cycle rites are not necessarily accompanied by recited myths in Bengal. Each life cycle rite has one or more deities who are central to the ritual observance, but the manner of the worship varies from house to house or from one caste to another. For an analysis of birth *strī ācār*s, see Fruzzetti, 1976.

18. Note also the following quote: "The ideal of *pativrata*, i.e., being devoted to the husband alone, popularized by the Puranic writers, not merely implied fidelity to the husband but made service to the husband the only duty of the wife, her only purpose in life (p. 69)." The woman's individuality is merged into that of the husband and his individuality is merged into that of the household and line as a whole.

BIBLIOGRAPHY

Baig, Tara Ali
1958 *Women of India*. Howrah: Glascow Printing.

Balfour, Edward (ed.)
1885 *The Cyclopaedia of India and of Eastern and Southern Asia*. 3rd ed. London: Bernard Quanth.

Barnett, S., L. Fruzzetti, and Á. Östör
1976 "Hierarchy Purified: Notes on Dumont and his Critics." *Journal of Asian Studies*, 35(4).

Berreman, Gerald D.
1972 *Hindus of the Himalayas*. 2nd ed. Berkeley and Los Angeles: University of California Press.

Bougle, Celestin
1971 *Essays on the Caste System* (ed. D. F. Pocock). Cambridge: Cambridge University Press.

Carstairs, M.
1957 *The Twice Born: A Study of a Community of High-caste Hindus*. London: Hogarth.

Carter, A. T.
1973 "A Comparative Analysis of Systems of Kinship and Marriage in South Asia." *Proceedings of the Royal Anthropological Institute of Great Britain*.

Chakraborty, D. Usha
1963 *Conditions of Bengali Women around the Second Half of the Nineteenth Century*. Calcutta: Bardhan.

Chattopadhyaya, D.
1964 *Indian Philosophy: A Popular Introduction*. New Delhi: People's Publishing.

Das, R. M.
1962 *Women in Manu and His Seven Commentators*. Varanasi: Kacchana.

David, K.
1974 "Until Marriage Do Us Part: A Cultural Account of Jaffna Tamil Categories for Kinsmen." *Man*, 8(3).

Dimock, Edward C.

1969 "Manasa, Goddess of Snakes: The Sasthi Myth." In J. Kitagawa and C. Long (eds.), *Myths and Symbols*. Chicago: University of Chicago Press.

Dimock, E. C., and A. K. Ramanujan

1964 "Manasa, Goddess of Snakes." *History of Religions*, 3(2).

Dowson, John

1961 (1888) *A Classical Dictionary of Hindu Mythology and Religion, Geography, History and Literature*. London: Routledge & Kegan Paul.

D'Souza, Victor S. (ed.)

1970 *All India Seminar on the Indian Family in the Change and Challenge of the Seventies*. New Delhi: Sterling.

Dumont, Louis

1953 "The Dravidian Kinship Terminology as an Expression of Marriage." *Man*, 53(article 54).

1957 "Hierarchy and Marriage Alliance in South Indian Kinship." (London) *Royal Anthropological Institute, Occasional Papers*, no. 12.

1959 "Pure and Impure." *Contributions to Indian Sociology*, no. 3.

1961 "Caste, Racism, and Stratification: Reflections of a Social Anthropologist." *Contributions to Indian Sociology*, no. 5.

1966 "Marriage in India: The Present State of the Question III: North India in Relation to South India." *Contributions to Indian Sociology*, no. 9.

1970a *Homo Hierarchicus: The Caste System and Its Implications*. Chicago: University of Chicago Press.

1970b *Religion, Politics and History in India*. The Hague: Mouton.

Ellickson, J.

1972 "Symbols in Muslim Bengali Family Rituals." (East Lansing, Michigan State University) *South Asian Center Occasional Papers*, no. 18.

Fallers, L. A. and Margaret C.

1976 "Sex Roles in Edremit." In J. Peristiany (ed.), *Mediterranean Family Structures*. Cambridge: Cambridge University Press.

Fonesca, M.

1963 "Family Disorganization and Divorce in Indian Communities." (Bombay) *Sociological Bulletin*, 12(2).

1964 "Marital Separation: Disorganization as Seen through an Agency." (Bombay) *Sociological Bulletin*, 13(1).

1966 *Counselling for Marital Happiness*. Bombay: Manaktalas.

Fruzzetti, Lina

1971 *The Social Organization of West Bengal Muslims.* M.A. Thesis, Department of Anthropology, University of Chicago.

1972 "The Idea of the Community among West Bengal Muslims." (East Lansing, Michigan State University) *South Asian Center Occasional Papers,* no. 18.

1976 "Food and Worship: An Analysis of Hindu and Muslim Birth Rituals." In Abid Ghazi (ed.), *Hindu and Muslim Interaction.* Manuscript.

1979 Review of R. Inden and R. W. Nicholas, *Kinship in Bengali Culture. American Anthropologist,* 81(4).

1980a "Muslim Rituals: Household Rites vs. Public Festivals." In Imtias Ahmed (ed.), *Indian Muslim Rituals.* New Delhi: Vikas Publishing.

1980b "Ritual Status of Muslim Women in Rural India." In Jane Smith (ed.), *Women in Contemporary Muslim Society.* Lewisburg, Pa.: Bucknell University Press.

Fruzzetti, L., and Á. Östör

1976a "Is There a Structure to North Indian Kinship Terminology? A Discussion of the Bengali Case." *Contributions to Indian Sociology,* n.s. 10(1).

1976b "The Seed and the Earth: A Cultural Analysis of Kinship in a Bengali Town." *Contributions to Indian Sociology,* n.s. 10(1).

Fruzzetti, L., Á. Östör, and S. Barnett

1976 "The Cultural Construction of the Person in Bengal and Tamilnadu." *Contributions to Indian Sociology,* n.s. 10(1).

Geertz, Clifford

1973 *The Interpretation of Culture.* New York: Basic Books.

Gough, E. Kathleen

1955 "Female Initiation Rites on the Malabar Coast." *Journal of the Royal Anthropological Institute,* 85.

1959 "The Nayars and the Definition of Marriage." *Journal of the Royal Anthropological Institute,* 89.

Gupta, Giri Raj

1974 *Marriage, Religion and Society.* New York: Wiley.

Hate, Chandrakala Anandrao

1969 *Changing Status of Women in Post Independence India.* New York: Paragon Book (reprint).

Inden, R.

1976 *Marriage and Rank in Bengali Culture.* Berkeley and Los Angeles: University of California Press.

Inden, R., and R. Nicholas
1977 *Kinship in Bengali Culture.* Chicago: University of Chicago Press.

Jones, V. R., and L. R. Jones
1941 *Women in Islam.* Lucknow: Lucknow Publishing.

Kannan, C. T.
1961 "Intercaste Marriage in Bombay." *Sociological Bulletin,* 10(2).
1963 *Intercaste and Intercommunity Marriages in India.* Bombay: Allied.

Kapadia, K. M.
1947 *Hindu Kinship.* Bombay: Popular Book Depot.
1958 *Marriage and Family in India.* Madras: Oxford University Press.
1966 *Marriage and Family in India.* 3rd ed. Madras: Oxford University Press.

Kapur, P.
1970 *Marriage and the Working Woman in India.* Delhi: Vikas Publishing.
1974 *The Changing Status of the Working Woman in India.* Delhi: Vikas Publishing.

Karve, I.
1965 *Kinship Organization in India.* 2nd ed. Bombay: Asia Publishing.

Khan, Mazhur ul Hag
1972 *Purdah and Polygamy.* Peshawar: Nashiren-e-Ibn-a-Taragiyet.

Khare, R. S.
1972 "Hierarchy and Hypergamy: Some Interrelated Aspects among the Kanya-Kubja Brahmans." *American Anthropologist,* 74(3).

Khawaja, B. A.
1965 "Attitudes Towards Purdah among Muslim Girl Students of Kanpur." *Man in India,* 45.

Lévi-Strauss, Claude
1966 *The Savage Mind.* London: Garden City.

Majumdar, R. R.
1971 *History of Ancient Bengal.* Calcutta: G. K. Mukerjee.

Marriott, M.
1966 "The Feast of Love." In Milton Singer (ed.), *Krishna: Myths, Rites and Attitudes.* Honolulu: East-West Centre Press.

Mathur, K. S.
1964 *Caste and Ritual in a Malwa Village.* Calcutta: Asia Publishing.

Mauss, Marcel

1967 *The Gift*. New York: Norton.

Misra, R.

1967 *Women in Noghal India*. New Delhi: M. O. Nunshiran.

Niaz, Hussain R.

1929 "The Purdah [veil] System amongst the Muslims of India." *Islamic Review*, 17.

Östör, Ákos

1980 *The Play of the Gods: Locality, Ideology, Structure, and the Festivals of a Bengali Town*. Chicago: University of Chicago Press.

Östör, Á., L. Fruzzetti, and S. Barnett (eds.)

1980 *Concepts of Person: Kinship, Caste and Marriage in India*. Cambridge, Mass.: Harvard University Press.

Papanek, Hanna

1973 "Purdah: Separate Worlds and Symbolic Shelter." *Comparative Studies in Society and History*, 5(3).

Peters, E.

1968 "Sex Differentiation in Two Arab Communities." Mimeo.

Pocock, D. F.

1957 "Inclusion and Exclusion: A Process in the Caste System of Gujarat." *Southwestern Journal of Anthropology*, 13.

1972 *Kanbi and Patidar: A Study of the Patidar Community on Gujarat*. London: Oxford University Press.

Ross, A.

1961 *The Hindu Family in Its Urban Setting*. Toronto: University of Toronto Press.

Schneider, D. M.

1968 *American Kinship: A Cultural Account*. Englewood Cliffs, N.J.: Prentice-Hall.

1972 "What Is Kinship All About?" In P. Reining (ed.), *Kinship Studies in the Morgan Centennial Year*. Washington: Anthropological Society of Washington.

1976 "Notes Towards a Theory of Culture." In K. Basso and H. Selby (eds.), *Meaning in Anthropology*. Albuquerque: University of New Mexico Press.

Shah, A. M.

1974 *The Household Dimension of the Family in India*. Berkeley and Los Angeles: University of California Press.

Siddigi, M. M.

1952 *Women in Islam*. Lahore: Institute of Islamic Culture.

Singer, M.
1968 "The Indian Joint Family in Modern Industry." In M. Singer and B. S. Cohn (ed.), *Structure and Change in Indian Society*. Chicago: Aldine.

Srinivas, M. N.
1942 *Marriage and Family in Mysore*. Bombay: New Book.
1966a *Religion and Society among the Coorgs of South India*. London: Oxford University Press.
1966b *Social Change in Modern India*. Berkeley and Los Angeles: University of California Press.

Stevenson, M. S.
1926 *The Rites of the Twice Born*. London: Oxford University Press.

Sur, Atal Krishna
1973 *Sex and Marriage in India: An Ethnohistorical Survey*. Bombay: Allied Publishing.

Tambiah, S. J.
1965 "Kinship Fact and Fiction in Relation to Kandyan Sinhalese." *Journal of Royal Anthropological Institute*, 95(pt. 2).
1973a "Dowry and Bridewealth and the Property Rights of Women in South Asia." In Jack Goody and S. J. Tambiah (eds.), *Bridewealth and Dowry*. Cambridge: Cambridge University Press.
1973b "From Varna to Caste through Mixed Unions." In Jack Goody (ed.), *Character of Kinship*. Cambridge: Cambridge University Press.

Thomas, P.
1939 *Women and Marriage in India*. London: George Allen & Unwin.
1964 *Women through the Ages*. Calcutta: Statesman.

Turner, Victor
1967 *The Forest of Symbols*. Ithaca, N.Y.: Cornell University Press.

Underhill, M. N.
1921 *The Hindu Ritual Year*. Calcutta: Association Press.

Urquhart, Margaret M.
1925 *Women of Bengal: A Study of the Hindu Pardnassins of Calcutta*. Calcutta: Association Press.

Van der Veen, Klaas W.
1972 *I Give Thee My Daughter: A Study of Marriage and Hierarchy among the Anavil Brahmans of S. Gujarat*. Assen: Van Gorcum.

Vatuk, S.

1969 "A Structural Analysis of the Hindu Kinship Terminology." *Contributions to Indian Sociology*, n.s. 3.

1975 "Gifts and Affines in North India." *Contributions to Indian Sociology*, n.s. 9.

Vreede de Steurs, Cora

1968 *Para: A Study of Muslim Women's Life in Northern India.* Assen: Van Gorcum.

Wadley, S.

1975 *Shakti: Power in the Conceptual Structures of Karimpur Religion.* Chicago: University of Chicago Press.

Yalman, Nur

1962 "The Structure of the Sinhalese Kindred: A Re-examination of the Dravidian Terminology." *American Anthropologist*, 64(3).

1963 "On the Purity of Women in the Castes of Ceylon and Malabar." *Journal of the Royal Anthropological Institute*, 93(pt. 1).

1967 *Under the Bo Tree: Studies in Caste, Kinship and Marriage in the Interior of Ceylon.* Berkeley and Los Angeles: University of California Press.

INDEX

Ācārs (rites, customs), 128. *See also* Marriage rituals; Rituals; *Strī ācārs*
Adopted boys, married women and, 23
Adoption: of daughter's son, 2; of male to perpetuate a line, 22; marriage and, 23
Adultery, 10
Alliance: hierarchal status and economic power in marriage, 132; marriage and, 37; woman's notion of, 15
Ālta (red lac dye), 50
Ancestoral deity (*kuladebatā*), 3, 101
Ancestors: male, 18; man's relationship to, 26; at marriage rites, 16, 51; marriage rules and, 113–114; offerings to, 19; rite honoring, 66–67; sacredness of, 13; *sapiṇḍa*, 114
Anthropological studies, 1, 142
Asian women, Western assumptions about position of, 2
Astrology, 33, 77, 155 n.18
Attiya grouping, 19–20, 22

Badha, 65, 156 n.1
Bangles, wearing of, 74–75. *See also names of specific kinds of bangles*
Baṅgśa: exchange of wives and daughters among, 20; perpetuation of, 24. *See also* Male line, relatives of
Barber, 43, 48–50; services of, in rituals, 88; touch of, 130
Basketmaker, 43
Baskets, 47
Bastra gift, 57–59
Bath: first after marriage, 50; widowhood, 105
Bathing rites and rituals, 70, 84–89
Beliefs: marriage rites and, 14–16
Bengali marriage (*biye*): alliance system of, 34–38; kinship and, 112–117; major elements of, 9
Bengali society: castes and marriage and, 9; understanding, 6
Bengali women. *See* Women; Women's rites and rituals; Women's world in India
Betel nuts, 70, 71
Bhāiyat, 18, 19; distinguished from *rakta*, 21; distinguishing factor for, 116; role of, 115
Bhakti (devotional love, sacred love), 12
Birth, 25, 101
Biye. *See* Bengali marriage
Blood, 120, 121; difference between marriage and adoption and, 23; line and, 23; as male, 22; shared, 26; ties of, 113–114, 115–117; transmission of categories by, 24
Blood relationships, 27
Blood relatives, 23; defined, 17
Brāhman: as cook, 130; as model for women's ritual action, 68; in *pūjā*, 69
Brāhmaṇas, 159 n.1
Brahmanical rites and rituals, 65, 121–122, 137–139; most important, 66; women's rituals and, 67–68
Brāhman priest: marriage rituals of lower castes and, 160 n.13; as ritualist, 69; and *stri ācārs* rites, 64, 66
Brāhman ritualists, 43, 66–69
Bratas, 102; *strī ācārs* and, 102, 122
Bride: acceptance of, 2, 58; change of *gotra* of, 43; child, 44; code of con-